■ New ambitions for our country:
A NEW CONTRACT FOR WELFARE

Presented to Parliament by
the Secretary of State for Social Security
and the Minister for Welfare Reform
by Command of Her Majesty
March 1998

Cm 3805

£11.50

Contents

iii Foreword and Introduction

1 Summary

9 Chapter One   The background to reform

17 Chapter Two   The four ages of welfare

23 Chapter Three   The importance of work

33 Chapter Four   New partnerships for welfare

43 Chapter Five   The importance of welfare services

51 Chapter Six   Support for disabled people

57 Chapter Seven   Support for families and children

63 Chapter Eight   Attacking social exclusion

67 Chapter Nine   Rooting out fraud

71 Chapter Ten   A modern service

79 Chapter Eleven   The fourth age: Welfare 2020

Appendix: The evolution of social security

Foreword and Introduction
from the Prime Minister

There has been no truly comprehensive review of the welfare state in all its elements since Beveridge. Individual benefits and contributions have been altered. But no one since then has attempted to survey the current system in its entirety, define its strengths and weaknesses and then lay out a political and intellectual framework for its reform and future development.

The result is not a blueprint for every benefit. This Green Paper marks the beginning of a debate, not its conclusion. We want it to be debated up and down the country, re-worked and refined, before we publish our proposals on the detail of the individual components of reform.

But the principles guiding reform and our vision of the future welfare state are clear. We want to rebuild the system around work and security. Work for those who can; security for those who cannot.

Substantial welfare reform is already happening. In the area of welfare to work, we have the New Deal, the largest assault on structural unemployment ever undertaken in this country, benefiting the young and long-term unemployed and, potentially, many lone parents, disabled people, and those with long-term illnesses. The Budget marked the first step in the transformation in how the tax and benefit system interacts with the world of work. The reform of student finance is the most important re-casting of the system for supporting our universities and students since higher education began to be extended beyond a small and privileged few. The radical alteration now proposed to our legal aid system, which will attempt to bring civil justice within the reach of ordinary citizens, is another.

For those of us who believe the welfare state is not just about cash benefits, but is about services too – like health and education – there are also hugely ambitious programmes of reform underway in our schools and hospitals.

Change can be controversial; and some of the ideas flagged up in this Green Paper will be too. Reform in areas such as pensions may stretch over decades, and is therefore a delicate political and administrative task. Our belief is that we should put in place a framework for reform, so that people can see the direction of reform and the shape of things to come. This will give confidence and security, enabling citizens and businesses to plan ahead. Reform is a vital part of rediscovering a true national purpose, part of a bigger picture in which our country is a model of the 21st century developed nation: with sound, stable economic management; dynamism and enterprise in business; the best educated and creative nation in the world; and a welfare state that promotes our aims and achievements.

We are acutely aware of the fears that even talk of welfare reform can arouse. For some, benefits are their lifeline. So we must approach reform sensitively and with the full engagement of the whole country.

But we should not forget why reform is right, and why, whatever the concerns over individual benefits, most people **know** it is right. Above all, the system must change because the world has changed, beyond the recognition of Beveridge's generation. The world of work has altered – people no longer expect a job for life; traditional industries have declined; new technologies have taken their place. There is a premium on skills and re-skilling throughout life. The role of women has been transformed. Family structures are different. We live longer, but work for fewer years. And the expectations of disabled people have changed out of all recognition, from half a century ago. We need a system designed not for yesterday, but for today.

But the welfare system has not kept pace with change. As a result, it is failing in its historical mission of creating a fairer and more prosperous society. There are three fundamental problems with the current system.

First, inequality has risen sharply and large numbers of people – particularly pensioners and children – are living in poverty. There are more homes of working age where no one works than would have been considered tolerable even 20 years ago. Yet the social security bill has risen far more than health or education. A system in which you spend more, but fail to stem urgent need, is plainly not working.

Secondly, the system all too often acts against those who want to work, creating a number of disincentives to move from benefits into the world of work. Disabled people, especially, face serious barriers to work.

Thirdly, the system urgently needs reform because it is open to abuse. While many people do not get the benefits they are entitled to, others take advantage of the system. It is not just fraud, though that is unacceptably widespread, for example in Housing Benefit. The rules themselves can be bent as well as broken, rewarding those who play the system.

The question is often put: are these changes going to be 'cuts-driven' or 'reform driven'? The answer is clear: they are driven by the need to reform: but of course, in reforming, we want to spend money in the fairest and most effective way. And in some cases, for example, for those severely disabled people with the greatest needs, or in our schools and hospitals, we will want to spend more. But in other cases, such as those who are socially excluded, we want to cut the cost of economic failure; not by lowering their standard of living but by raising their life chances. So we must have a system we can afford, but above all, we want a system that aids those who need it and helps people to help themselves.

We must return to first principles and ask what we want the welfare state to achieve. This is the question this Green Paper seeks to answer. In essence, it describes a third way: not dismantling welfare, leaving it simply as a low-grade safety net for the destitute; nor keeping it unreformed and underperforming; but reforming it on the basis of a new contract between citizen and state, where we keep a welfare state from which we all benefit, but on terms that are fair and clear.

There is a very simple reason why we need such a contract more than ever today. The welfare state we have is one from which the vast majority of us benefit through a state pension or Child Benefit or use of the NHS. The welfare state isn't just about a few benefits paid to the most needy.

But we all contribute through taxes and charges. We benefit but we pay. It is a contract between us as citizens. As such, it needs to be a fair deal, within a system that is clearer, more relevant for the modern world, efficiently run and where costs are manageable. One that is fair not just for the existing generation, but fair between the generations.

That is the fundamental reason for reform. It will take time. Frank Field has started the process in this Green Paper. Now that the process is underway, we want all the nation to be part of it. There will be consultation and time for discussion at every stage. Our objective is to build a genuine national consensus behind change. The welfare state belongs to us all. It is part of our inheritance. We must now all work together to re-build it for the new century that awaits.

Tony Blair

Prime Minister

Summary

A brief outline of this Green Paper

CHAPTER ONE : THE BACKGROUND TO REFORM

1. The welfare state was born 50 years ago. At its birth, the vision was broad and encompassed all welfare services, such as education and health as well as social security benefits. We need to recapture that original vision. The existing system needs reform. For many people the system is increasing their dependence on benefit, rather than helping them to lead independent and fulfilling lives.

2. There are three key problems with the existing system:

- **inequality and social exclusion are worsening, especially among children and pensioners, despite rising spending on social security;**

- **people face a series of barriers to paid work, including financial disincentives; and**

- **fraud is taking money out of the system and away from genuine claimants.**

3. The United Kingdom (UK) has seen profound economic changes in recent decades, for example: the gap between those on highest and lowest earnings has widened; many jobs have become less secure; women have entered the workforce in increasing numbers; and the number of households in which no one has a job has grown.

4. Society has changed too. An ageing population has created new pressures on pensions and long-term care provision. Families are also changing, with more divorce and separation, and a rising number of single parents. Voters and consumers have become more demanding, with rising expectations of quality services. Yet some people, the socially excluded, are so afflicted by unemployment and deprivation that they no longer participate fully in society.

CHAPTER TWO : THE FOUR AGES OF WELFARE

5. Change is not new; the structure of social security provision has evolved over centuries. In the early stage, welfare was concerned with stopping outright destitution. Its second stage focused on alleviating poverty through insurance-based cash benefit systems. The welfare state now faces a choice of three futures:

- **a privatised future with the welfare state becoming a residual safety net for the poorest and most marginalised; or**

- **the *status quo* but with more generous and costly benefits; or**

- **the Government's third way – promoting opportunity instead of dependence, with the welfare state for the broad mass of people, but in new ways to fit the modern world.**

6 This third way will take us into the third stage of welfare. The welfare system will become pro-active, preventing poverty by ensuring that people have the right education, training and support. We will widen the exits from welfare dependency by offering tailor-made help for individuals.

7 Eight key principles will guide our reform programme:

- **The new welfare state should help and encourage people of working age to work where they are capable of doing so.**

- **The public and private sectors should work in partnership to ensure that, wherever possible, people are insured against foreseeable risks and make provision for their retirement.**

- **The new welfare state should provide public services of high quality to the whole community, as well as cash benefits.**

- **Those who are disabled should get the support they need to lead a fulfilling life with dignity.**

- **The system should support families and children, as well as tackling the scourge of child poverty.**

- **There should be specific action to attack social exclusion and help those in poverty.**

- **The system should encourage openness and honesty and the gateways to benefit should be clear and enforceable.**

- **The system of delivering modern welfare should be flexible, efficient and easy for people to use.**

8 The Government is determined to put these principles into action and be held to account. **Chapters Three** to **Ten** set out a series of success measures to be achieved over the next 10-20 years. These are listed in full at the end of **Chapter Eleven** which describes the Fourth Age of welfare that we will then have entered.

CHAPTER THREE : THE IMPORTANCE OF WORK

9   Work is at the heart of our reform programme. For those able to undertake it, paid work is the surest route out of poverty. A pay packet also gives people independence and status in the community, and the chance to insure against risk and save for retirement. But one in five working age households have no one in work and youth unemployment is unacceptably high. These are the areas where we must target our efforts.

10 There are five elements to the Government's attack on worklessness.

- Introducing a direct programme of help to key groups through the New Deal, rebuilding welfare around the work ethic backed up by Employment Zones. Young people, lone parents, the long-term unemployed, and people who are disabled or have a long-term illness will be the beneficiaries.

- Developing an individualised, flexible service for those out of work with personal advisers providing tailor-made packages of help.

- Tackling the barriers to work faced by workless households, including low skills, fears about the time lag between benefits and wages, the perverse incentives which discourage people from moving from benefits to work and the lack of access to affordable childcare.

- Ensuring that work pays. The proposed Working Families Tax Credit offers more generous support to working families; lower taxes for lower-paid workers will improve incentives; the proposed national minimum wage will ensure fair pay; and a modernised National Insurance scheme will promote work and cut red tape.

- Changing the nature of the relationship between government and claimant. It is the responsibility of government to provide positive help; it is the responsibility of claimants to take it up.

CHAPTER FOUR : NEW PARTNERSHIPS FOR WELFARE

11 We need higher levels of saving to provide decent retirement incomes – that is the hard reality. And we need to recognise the significant differences in pensioner incomes. We can only tackle these issues by combining public and private sector provision. Pension provision needs to increase, but the proportion financed by taxpayers will not, as measures such as Stakeholder Pensions will provide greater private cover. We are also considering whether further measures are needed to ensure greater saving for retirement. And we must do more to get help to the poorest pensioners.

12 Many people already benefit from private provision on top of state-funded pensions, but those people stuck in a cycle of lower paid work and unemployment are losing out. So are carers. Our proposals for Stakeholder Pensions will give wider access to a portable, second-tier pension. We are also examining the creation of Citizenship Pensions. In addition, the system of regulation requires further strengthening to improve the security and performance of private pensions. We will also encourage people on low incomes to save more through Individual Savings Accounts.

13 One million pensioners fail to take up their full benefit entitlement. A programme of reform to ensure take-up will be undertaken. This will begin with a series of pilot exercises to improve take-up, including customer-friendly means of contact, as well as targeted help for pensioners.

14 We have set up a Royal Commission on long-term care which will report by early next year. We will also examine how to improve protection for home owners with mortgages, while ensuring that those people who take out insurance on credit agreements are not penalised.

CHAPTER FIVE : THE IMPORTANCE OF WELFARE SERVICES

15 Services – especially education, health and housing – are at least as important as cash benefits in promoting independence and security; tackling poverty and widening opportunity.

16 A skilled workforce is essential to a modern economy, and high educational standards offer people their best chance of a secure and prosperous life. This Government is committed to raising standards in schools; to promoting life-long learning; and to widening access to higher education.

17 The National Health Service (NHS) is being modernised to improve standards. The Government will also publish a White Paper later this year, setting out proposals for social services.

18 While most people own their own homes there is still a signficant need for a quality rented sector and for help with rent for those on low incomes. The welfare state has to assist in this aim. The present system of Housing Benefit is open to abuse and, in addition, local government and housing associations often encounter problems in improving the quality of housing. We are conducting a comprehensive review of housing support.

CHAPTER SIX : SUPPORT FOR DISABLED PEOPLE

19 Disabled people face a range of social and economic disadvantages, not least in the area of civil rights. A Disability Rights Task Force has been set up, and a Disability Rights Commission will be established to protect, enforce and promote the rights of disabled people. In addition, we will implement the remaining provisions of the Disability Discrimination Act. We are also introducing the New Deal for Disabled People.

20 Incapacity Benefit should be reformed fundamentally for future claimants. We are examining the scope for a more effective test for new claimants which will assess the extent of their employability. Disability Living Allowance and Attendance Allowance will remain national, universal benefits for all those who meet the entitlement conditions. However, we will work with disability groups to introduce better and clearer gateways. Our aim is to reduce spending on Incapacity Benefit and to increase it for those severely disabled people with the greatest needs. In addition, we are reforming the Benefits Integrity Project which has not worked satisfactorily, in consultation with disabled people.

CHAPTER SEVEN : SUPPORT FOR FAMILIES AND CHILDREN

21 One in three children lives in a household with an income below half the average. Although the family remains a fundamental building block of society, it is often children and families who bear the brunt of economic change. As announced in the Budget, we will increase support for families across the country, as well as help given to poorer families, by increasing Child Benefit and the children's rates for those aged under 11 in Income Support and the other income-related benefits.

22 The Government will help parents into the labour market through the Childcare Tax Credit within the Working Families Tax Credit, better childcare provision and the extension of family-friendly working practices. One million children and their parents will be helped over the next five years by the Government's national childcare network. Strategies to reduce the number of teenage conceptions, including better education, will be put in place.

23 Parents should support their children, but the Child Support Agency (CSA) is failing to tackle this issue effectively. Proper maintenance is only secured in a third of cases, and delay and complexity bedevil the system. We will announce proposals for fundamental reform of the CSA later this year.

24 Teenage conceptions in the UK are among the highest in Europe and are increasing. Deprived areas are characterised by especially high rates. Our planned Healthy Schools Initiative will aim to improve school children's knowledge of responsible relationships and good parenting, so as to reduce the rate of conceptions among those aged under 16, with a set of local targets in the areas most affected.

CHAPTER EIGHT : ATTACKING SOCIAL EXCLUSION

25 Concerted action will be taken to tackle social exclusion. Action Zones for education, health and employment will all target resources on deprived areas, fitting services to local needs. The New Deal for Communities will help to provide employment opportunities for those in the worst estates. Social exclusion will be addressed at its roots, through programmes to reduce truancy and rough sleeping, and new integrated and sustainable solutions for areas facing particularly severe problems, including crime, drugs and unemployment.

CHAPTER NINE : ROOTING OUT FRAUD

26 Fraud undermines the social security system and erodes public confidence. The estimated £4 billion lost each year could provide every family with an extra £10 a week. We will improve detection with better co-ordination between agencies, especially to target widespread Housing Benefit fraud. We will impose more effective sanctions to deter people from trying to commit fraud. And, in the longer term, we will aim to prevent it by designing benefit systems to minimise the scope for fraud.

CHAPTER TEN : A MODERN SERVICE

27 We are determined to build an Active Modern Service, providing positive help into work and delivering an efficient and straightforward service to everyone – whether they are able to work or not. We plan to increase the number of personal advisers who can identify individual needs for training, work placements and childcare. We will put customers at the centre of service delivery.

28 In order to transform our service, we will improve support for front-line staff. As our biggest asset, they are at the forefront of new ideas for improvement. We will improve co-ordination, especially between benefit offices, Jobcentres and local authorities. New technology and new ways of working will be introduced to improve the system.

CHAPTER ELEVEN : THE FOURTH AGE: WELFARE 2020

29 By 2020, there should be in place a **new welfare contract** between the citizens of the country and the Government. This will deliver greater trust, transparency, responsibility and responsiveness and people will be empowered to seize the opportunities to lead independent lives.

30 Welfare will be provided by three channels: our Active Modern Service, based on a single work-focused gateway into the benefit system; mutual organisations and private providers, delivering a substantial share of welfare provision, particularly for pensioners; and high-quality health, education and other welfare services.

CONCLUSION

31 This Green Paper sets out the framework for welfare reform, based on eight principles, together with a range of success measures which will help to guide progress over a 10 to 20 year time horizon. Reform will not be quick or easy. But it is vital that we start the process now. It is also vital that reform is informed by a full debate on the proposed framework. We are consulting widely on the contents of this Green Paper and we want your views. For instance, how can we best deliver on our guiding principles? Are there ways in which the policy direction can be improved? Are our tracking measurements for success right?

32 Please write to the following address:

The Welfare Reform Green Paper Consultation Team
Department of Social Security
7th Floor, The Adelphi
1-11 John Adam Street
London WC2N 6HT

You can also respond by using the following email address:
welfarereform@ade001.dss.gov.uk

Comments should reach us by 31 July 1998.

33 This Green Paper is also available in Braille, audio cassette and in Welsh (Cmd 3805, price £11.50), from Stationery Office bookshops. A list of their bookshops is given on the back of this publication. In addition, a summary version has been produced and is available free of charge from the following address:

Welfare Reform
Freepost (HA4441)
Hayes
UB3 1BR

Chapter One

The background to reform

1   The welfare state is 50 years old this year. Conceived during the darkest days of the Second World War, it was established with the most noble aims:

> *"The scheme as a whole will embrace, not certain occupations and income groups, but the entire population. Concrete expression is thus given to the solidarity and unity of the nation, which in war have been its bulwarks against aggression and in peace will be its guarantees of success in the fight against individual want and mischance."*
> (Social Insurance, Cmd 6550 [1944])

2   Comprehensive insurance and a universal safety-net were intended to prevent any citizen from falling into poverty. Even though incomes were low in the aftermath of the war, the National Insurance and National Assistance schemes meant that no one went without at least a basic share. The creation of the National Health Service ensured that all individuals would be provided with free and comprehensive medical care. The principles of fairness and solidarity which were the bedrock of the schemes were envied across the world. Over the last 50 years, they have proved their lasting value.

3   But the welfare system has failed to keep pace with profound economic, social and political changes. The machinery of welfare has the air of yesteryear. As the first part of this chapter shows, it often fails to offer the kind of support needed in today's world. It chains people to passive dependency instead of helping them to realise their full potential. The second part of this chapter examines the areas of change – social, political and economic – which have shaped the modern world, and which the Government must take into account.

4   Welfare reform does not simply mean improving social security. As William Beveridge noted, *"Want is one only of five giants on the road to reconstruction and in some ways the easiest to attack. The others are Disease, Ignorance, Squalor and Idleness"*. The welfare system involves health, education, housing and employment as well as social security and we plan significant reforms in those areas too.

■ PROBLEMS WITH THE CURRENT SYSTEM

5   The current social security system has three fundamental problems.

- **Increased inequality and social exclusion, despite more spending.**

- **People are trapped on benefit rather than being helped off.**

- **Fraud is diverting resources from genuine claimants.**

Increased inequality and social exclusion

6   Society has become more fragmented. While the majority of the population has become more prosperous over the last two decades, some families and communities have been cut off from the mainstream.

- **Between 1979 and 1994/95, households in the top fifth of the population saw income rises in excess of 50 per cent; but the incomes of those in the bottom fifth barely rose in real terms.**

7   The rise in inequality has been particularly marked among pensioners. But, in general, the prospects of a decent income have improved significantly; being old no longer always equates to being poor.

- **The rising prosperity of pensioners has reduced the number relying on means-tested benefits, from 55 per cent in 1979 to 36 per cent in 1994/95.**

8   Inequality has also risen among people of working age. While the proportion of working age people in employment is about the same today as it was in 1979, more people live in households with no one in work. These households are more likely to be reliant on benefits and managing on a low income. Children have been hit hardest by the rise in the number of workless households.

- **Almost one in five working age households have no breadwinner compared to less than one in ten in 1979.**

- **Nearly three million children are growing up in workless households.**

9   There are three main reasons for the increase in worklessness. First, a general rise in unemployment, particularly male unemployment. Second, a rise in the number of working age men who are not officially unemployed, but are nonetheless out of the labour market – or 'economically inactive'. Third, the growth in households headed by a single adult – often a single parent.

10 Other factors have also fuelled the rise in the number of workless households. Couples often have similar skills and experience, so both partners may find themselves out of work if the local labour market takes a turn for the worse. Perverse incentives in the benefit system can also mean that when one partner loses a job, the other also gives up work.

11 Worklessness has become more geographically concentrated in urban areas. Unemployed or poor households are increasingly likely to live in communities with high levels of unemployment and benefit dependency. Some local labour markets, especially those in the inner cities or in areas dependent on declining traditional industries, have collapsed. During the 1980s, the main job losses were in the major cities, with particular estates being the hardest hit. As a result of these changes, whole communities have become cut off from the world of work.

- **73 per cent of all working age adults are in work, but in some deprived urban areas this falls to below 60 per cent – 59 per cent in Newcastle, 58 per cent in Liverpool and Glasgow, 53 per cent in Manchester, and 52 per cent in Tower Hamlets, in London.**

12 In areas bearing the brunt of long-term benefit dependency and worklessness, educational standards falter, crime rises and disillusionment sets in. Once a certain locality develops a reputation as a 'bad area', it becomes even harder for residents to secure a job. These areas also have a much higher proportion of housing in serious disrepair and of unfit dwellings with failing health and safety standards.

13 Along with income, death rates have become more polarised. In some deprived areas, infant mortality rates have failed to fall in line with national trends. The link between poverty and ill health is clear. In nearly every case, the highest incidence of illness is experienced by poorer people.

- **Between 1987 and 1991, the life expectancy of men in professional and managerial jobs was 75 years, compared with 70 years for those in partly skilled and unskilled occupations.**

14 This rise in inequality and social exclusion has occurred despite the growth in resources channelled into social security.

- **Over the last 50 years, the bill for social security has risen, in real terms, almost eight-fold.**

- **In 1949, spending on social security was around £12 billion at 1996/97 prices, 14 per cent of all government spending. It is forecast to be almost £100 billion next year, representing one third of all government spending.**

- **Between 1978/79 and 1996/97, spending on social security, in real terms, rose by 4 per cent a year, a faster rate of growth than any other major area of government expenditure, including health and education.**

- **The cost of the social security budget is now the equivalent of almost £80 every week for every household in the country.**

The benefit trap

15 At present, the welfare state concentrates on supporting people rather than helping people to support themselves. While the rules of some benefits require some claimants to look for work, and in return offer them help to do so, others fail to encourage other groups of claimants to enter the labour market, or to undertake training or voluntary work. For example, lone mothers awarded benefit have been effectively written off until their youngest child is aged 16. In addition, people are sometimes no better off financially in paid work than on the dole. Benefits are often withdrawn so quickly as earnings come in that the family sees relatively little real increase in living standards.

- **Prior to the implementation of the reforms announced in the Budget, 740,000 people lost 70p of every extra £1 they earned because of benefit withdrawal. 130,000 families gained less than 10p for every extra £1 earned.**

16 In households with two working adults, the loss of a job for one can sometimes make a decision by the other to remain in work one which makes the family worse off. Low wages and anxieties about the time lag between the last benefit payment and first pay cheque can also erode incentives to enter employment.

- **Almost one in seven people who had moved from welfare to work said they were worse off in work than unemployed.**

17 One problem is that many individuals are not aware of the full range of in-work support available to low-paid workers, particularly Housing Benefit and Council Tax Benefit. They worry about meeting their housing costs if they find a job, unaware that help will still be available to them if they are on a low income.

18 Disabled people face particular difficulties in getting back into the labour market. Even where a job is available, disabled people may be discriminated against or be prevented by inaccessible transport from travelling to work.

- **Disabled people are twice as likely to be unemployed as anyone else, and studies have shown that equally qualified disabled applicants are less likely to be offered job interviews.**

19 Moreover, a gateway to Incapacity Benefit – the All Work Test – can have perverse effects. It is an 'all or nothing' test: people who pass are not expected to look for any kind of work, even of a different nature to their old job. As a result, some people who would be able to work again – with the kind of job assistance available to the registered unemployed – can end up spending the rest of their working life on benefit.

Fraud

20 The vast majority of social security claimants are honest. Nevertheless, fraud takes money away from genuine claimants and undermines public support for the system.

- **Fraud costs the taxpayer an estimated £4 billion every year – enough to give every family with children an extra £10 a week.**

- **One in four people say they know someone who has defrauded the social security system.**

■ THE CHANGING CONTEXT

Changing work

21 In large part, the system is failing because it has not kept pace with profound economic and social changes. The labour market has changed substantially in the last 50 years with more service and part-time jobs and fewer manual and full-time jobs. At the same time, the rewards for skills have grown, fuelling a widening pay gap.

- **The average gross weekly earnings of an individual with no qualifications is £240; compared to £470 for an individual with a degree.**

- **19 per cent of those unemployed for less than a year have no qualifications, but this rises to 40 per cent of those unemployed for more than two years. Only 13 per cent of those in employment have no qualifications.**

Working women

22 The process of modernising welfare has to accommodate new patterns of work and care. The welfare state based around the male breadwinner is increasingly out of date. While employment rates among men have been dropping, women have been entering the labour force in greater numbers.

- **The proportion of women of working age in employment rose from 59 per cent in 1973 to 67 per cent in 1995.**

Changing families

23 The family is the bedrock of a decent, civilised and stable society. But, it is under enormous strain. Divorce and separation have increased, lone parenthood has risen and child poverty has worsened. The reasons for this may be varied, but the impact is clear: more instability, more crime, greater pressure on housing and benefits.

24 Divorce rates have risen sharply in recent years, affecting the lives of thousands of children.

- **Between 1971 and 1995, the number of divorces in England and Wales doubled from 74,000 to 155,000 a year - after already doubling in the 1960s.**

- **One in four children born in the 1970s has witnessed the break-up of their parents' marriage.**

25 Over the last three decades, partly as a result of these changes, there has been a substantial increase in the number of lone parents.

- **In 1995, the proportion of families with dependent children with only one parent in the home was 22 per cent, compared to 8 per cent in 1971.**

- **One in five families is now headed by a lone parent: almost three times the proportion 25 years ago.**

26 The causes of lone parenthood have altered. Few lone parents are widows. During the 1970s, the main increase was in the number of divorced women with children. During the last decade, the most substantial growth has been in never married lone mothers, including a large number whose cohabiting partnerships have ended. Never married lone mothers are typically younger, with younger children, and with lower qualifications and job prospects than lone parents as a whole.

The ageing society

27 There are more elderly people today than 50 years ago. Each working person has to provide for more pensioners. And rising life expectancy is likely to lead to more people needing long-term care.

- **In 1953, there were 4.6 people of working age for every pensioner. Today, there are 3.4 and by 2040, the ratio will have dropped to just 2.4, even allowing for the equalisation of the retirement age.**

Disabled people and disability benefits: the changing picture

28 The number of people claiming disability benefits has risen in recent years.

- **The number of people claiming Incapacity Benefit has tripled to one and three-quarter million claimants over the last 20 years.**

- **The number claiming Disability Living Allowance and Attendance Allowance – which help with the costs of disability – has increased from two million to almost three million since 1993.**

29 In part, this reflects long-term trends, such as the significant increase in the life expectancy of disabled people and the general ageing of the population.

- **Two-thirds of disabled people are over retirement age.**

30   But other factors have also driven the growth in the number of claimants, including:

- **the shift in the balance of state support away from care in long stay hospitals (services) towards care in the community (supported by social security benefits);**

- **increasing numbers taking up the benefit;**

- **extended eligibility for benefit, partly as a result of court judgements.**

Increased individual and collective welfare provision

31   For those who have prospered in the changing labour market, new opportunities for welfare provision have opened up with the development of public/private partnerships. In 1953, only 28 per cent of employees were in an occupational pension scheme. Today, occupational schemes are the norm rather than the exception.

- **19 million workers, over three-quarters of the number in work, are building up funds in either an occupational or personal pension.**

- **More than £30 billion is being put into pensions by employees and employers every year. Even more is put aside if the contribution of taxpayers is included.**

32   Increased pension provision over and above government support has been a key factor behind rising general pensioner incomes. Insurance against death, sickness or disability has also grown in importance.

- **In 1995, two-thirds of households had some life insurance, providing for an average lump sum cover of £12,000.**

- **Almost one and a half million individuals have taken out insurance policies for incapacity.**

- **Nine out of ten employees are now given cover for sick pay by their employers.**

33   It is clear that while the state has a crucial role to play in the provision of financial welfare, employers, private-sector financial institutions, trade unions, mutual organisations and friendly societies are all important partners.

- **Friendly societies currently have assets of over £8 billion under their management and have more members than all of the UK's trade unions put together.**

34 Voluntary organisations are also a vital part of the welfare mix, either providing services alone or in partnership with government. Historically, voluntary provision has led and encouraged government provision. Today, government and the voluntary sector act in unison to maximise help for those in need.

35 Charities, good neighbour schemes and credit unions all make an enormous contribution to society. In many cases, voluntary agencies provide services directly: hostels for the homeless, day-clubs for the elderly, or support for mentally ill people. In other cases, the Government acts in concert with civic institutions: meals-on-wheels is a classic example of a government-voluntary sector partnership.

Rising expectations

36 Society has become more demanding. Consumers expect ever higher levels of service and better value for money. Voters want politicians who are accountable. Taxpayers want public agencies which meet their objectives efficiently. The *way* in which a service is delivered can be as important as the service itself - as retailers know only too well.

37 Three trends highlight the rise of the demanding, sceptical, citizen-consumer. First, confidence in the institutions of government and politics has tumbled. Second, expectations of service quality and convenience have risen – as with the growth in 24-hour banking – but public services have failed to keep up with these developments; their duplication, inefficiency, and unnecessary complexity should not be tolerated. Third, as incomes rise, people prefer to own their own homes and investments.

38 This chapter has charted the nature and scale of the challenge facing welfare reform. The Government is determined to build an active welfare system which helps people to help themselves and ensures a proper level of support in times of need.

Chapter Two

The four ages of welfare

1   The future direction of welfare is best judged by looking at how the current system came about. This chapter is about the evolution of social security and the choice of futures that face the nation.

2   A number of lessons about the direction of welfare reform can be drawn from the history of social security (which is described in more detail in the **Appendix**):

- **firstly, change is anything but new. The last 400 years have been characterised by a series of major advances;**

- **secondly, social security changes have long-term consequences. A quarter of a million of today's pensioners began their working life before the first contributory pensions were introduced in 1925. Contributions made today by a 16 year-old may affect his or her income in retirement in 70 years time; and**

- **thirdly, and most importantly, improvement requires change. Social security has to develop to meet the changing needs of each generation. But change does not necessarily imply sudden, large-scale shifts in direction. There is rarely a 'Big Bang' solution to the problems of the system.**

3   The four ages of welfare can be defined as:

- **the Poor Law – stopping outright destitution;**

- **the beginnings of the welfare state – alleviating poverty;**

- **preventing poverty – the stage on which we are now embarked; and**

- **promoting opportunity and developing potential – the stage to which we aspire.**

The First Age: The Poor Law – stopping outright destitution

4   In its infancy, welfare was concerned exclusively with tackling outright destitution. Four hundred years ago – in 1598 and 1601 – the Elizabethan Poor Laws were enacted in England and Wales. Though obviously inadequate and sometimes cruel in their application, these laws established several key principles.

- **The state had a responsibility to prevent destitution, raise taxes to do so and ensure that an administrative framework was in operation to deliver help.**

- **There was an important distinction between those who were unable to work, and people who were capable of independence but who were jobless.**

- **Assistance offered to those who were able to work should be conditional.**

The Poor Law, however, was not the only weapon against destitution. Private charity often played a more important role.

The Second Age: the birth of the welfare state – alleviating poverty

5   The next stage accompanied the inexorable rise in national income. As national wealth expanded, opinion changed about what was right and possible for welfare provision to achieve. Welfare became concerned with the alleviation of poverty, rather than acting merely as a road block against destitution. The provision of help became focused on assisting people to survive the vagaries of life and unexpected hardship. It became part of the growing belief in collective action to advance individual opportunity and security.

6   The main staging posts in the Second Age were:

- **old age pensions in 1908 and Lloyd George's 1911 sickness and unemployment insurance provisions;**

- **Neville Chamberlain's widows, orphans and old age pension coverage of 1925;**

- **Beveridge's National Insurance proposals; and**

- **non-contributory coverage for disabled people, regardless of means. This came with Keith Joseph's Attendance Allowance provisions in 1971 – for people who require care and attention because of their disability – and later, in 1976, with Barbara Castle's Mobility Allowance – for people who have difficulty in walking.**

7   It was the 1945–51 Government which laid the foundation stones of the welfare state in its broadest sense, establishing the National Health Service (NHS) and a wider education system, as well as the reforms to the benefit system, expanding pre-war provision to cover more of the population. Sir William Beveridge's great success was to bring together a series of disparate arrangements and give them coherence.

8   His aim was to replace the existing schemes with a unified system of social insurance, based on flat-rate benefits for flat-rate contributions and covering the whole population rather than only lower earners. The central aim was to supply a subsistence income during all the contingencies which interrupt earnings.

9   The lasting importance of his work has not been so much in the detailed prescriptions, which because of social and economic change are in some cases now out of date, but his enduring vision of the possibility of common action to defeat the great giants of *Want, Disease, Ignorance, Squalor* and *Idleness*. He saw clearly that financial support was not sufficient in itself to tackle the problems of poverty and distress. In the intervening 50 years, the country has seen itself that cash hand outs alone can lead to a life of dependency.

The Third Age: preventing poverty

10 The welfare state now faces a choice of futures. A privatised future, with the welfare state becoming a residual safety net for the poorest and most marginalised; the *status quo*, but with more generous benefits; or the Government's third way – promoting opportunity instead of dependence, with a welfare state providing for the mass of the people, but in new ways to fit the modern world. This is the choice for the nation.

11 The first future has its advocates among those who believe the concept of welfare is wrong. These people say that the welfare state is unaffordable, that it needs to be scaled back. The middle class should provide for themselves with little or no state cash or services. Unemployment, disability benefits and pensions should be fully privatised. These people believe that welfare went wrong when government became involved; that charity, however haphazard, is better than a state-run system. We believe that this is the route to a divided society – one side on benefit, the other paying for it. Political support for the welfare state would diminish and it would end up as a poor system for poor people.

12 The second future is supported by those who believe that any changes to the Beveridge system are a betrayal of his vision, even though the world has changed so dramatically. They believe that cash is the answer to most of the problems, that poverty is alleviated by more money rather than more opportunity. They defend the *status quo*, but want benefits for all to be more generous. They believe that poverty is relieved exclusively by cash hand outs.

13 This Government rejects both approaches. The first leaves the welfare state to disintegrate, fails to address poverty and leaves those on middle incomes more insecure. The second leads to rising bills and more people trapped in poverty. We propose a third way. A modern form of welfare that believes in empowerment not dependency. We believe that work is the best route out of poverty for those who can work. We believe in ensuring dignity and security for those who are unable to work because of disability or because of caring responsibilities, as well as for those who have retired. This system is about combining public and private provision in a new partnership for the new age.

14 Modern welfare goes beyond the limited, but important, role of stopping destitution. Nor is it simply concerned with alleviating poverty – although, of course, it still has that function as in any civilised society. And welfare is not only about acting after events have occurred. Where appropriate, the welfare system should be proactive, preventing poverty by ensuring that people have the right education, training and support to make provision for themselves. But, where there is poverty, the new welfare system must extend the exits from welfare dependency, moving from a mass-production service, which merely pays benefit, to one offering a professional, tailor-made service for each individual. That means giving people the chance to fulfil their potential.

15 The Government's approach has eight key principles.

- **The new welfare state should help and encourage people of working age to work where they are capable of doing so.**

- **The public and private sectors should work in partnership to ensure that, wherever possible, people are insured against foreseeable risks and make provision for their retirement.**

- **The new welfare state should provide public services of high quality to the whole community, as well as cash benefits.**

- **Those who are disabled should get the support they need to lead a fulfilling life with dignity.**

- **The system should support families and children, as well as tackling the scourge of child poverty.**

- **There should be specific action to attack social exclusion and help those in poverty.**

- **The system should encourage openness and honesty and the gateways to benefit should be clear and enforceable.**

- **The system of delivering modern welfare should be flexible, efficient and easy for people to use.**

16 Reform will not be big bang. It will be evolutionary. Each stage of policy development will be consulted on in full.

The Fourth Age: promoting opportunity and developing potential

17 Once our reform programme is fully in place, the new welfare contract between government and the people will give all of our citizens the means to achieve their full potential. Much more will be involved here than ensuring a person can gain work. A person who gains minimum qualifications will often secure an income which prevents poverty – in itself a worthy goal. But it is not enough. If someone gets and keeps a job that lifts them off the benefit book, but uses just a fraction of their skills and talents, is that the end of our responsibility? Not in the view of this Government. Welfare has to move beyond the provision of minimum standards.

18 The next eight chapters explain in more detail each of the principles underpinning our approach.

Chapter Three

The importance of work

> ### Principle One
> The new welfare state should help and encourage people of working age to work where they are capable of doing so.

1. The Government's aim is to rebuild the welfare state around work. The skills and energies of the workforce are the UK's biggest economic asset. And for both individuals and families, paid work is the most secure means of averting poverty and dependence except, of course, for those who are retired or so sick or disabled, or so heavily engaged in caring activities, that they cannot realistically support themselves.

2. For many people the absence of paid work is a guarantee of a life on low income. One of the reasons children make up a higher proportion of those at the bottom of the income distribution is that a growing number of parents, especially lone parents, are out of work. Paid work also allows people to save for their retirement.

3. For too long, governments have abandoned people to a life on benefits. Far too many individuals and families are penalised, or gain too little, if they move from benefit to work.

4. **Chapter One** described how work has changed over the last 50 years. The rewards for skills have grown, widening the wage gap. Some people reap the rewards of fairly paid work, while others are either stuck on benefit or switching between benefit dependency and short-term, low-skilled jobs. There has also been a shift in balance from full-time manual jobs to part-time and service-sector posts. In households with two working adults, the loss of a job for one can mean that the other would be better off giving up work too.

5. The Government aims to promote work by:

- **helping people move from welfare to work through the New Deals and Employment Zones;**

- **developing flexible personalised services to help people into work;**

- **lowering the barriers to work for those who can and want to work;**

- **making work pay, by reforming the tax and benefit system, including a Working Families Tax Credit, reforming National Insurance and income tax, and introducing the national minimum wage; and**

- **ensuring that responsibilities and rights are fairly matched.**

■ POLICY DIRECTION

Welfare to Work – The New Deals

6   The Government's biggest investment since taking office has been in a large-scale **welfare to work** programme. Our ambition is nothing less than a change of culture among benefit claimants, employers and public servants – with rights and responsibilities on all sides. Those making the shift from welfare into work will be provided with positive assistance, not just a benefit payment.

7   Our comprehensive welfare to work programme aims to break the mould of the old, passive benefit system. It is centred on the five aspects of the New Deal for:

- **young unemployed people;**
- **long-term unemployed people;**
- **lone parents;**
- **people with a disability or long-term illness; and**
- **partners of the unemployed.**

8   Alongside these national programmes, we are also piloting targeted help for areas of high long-term unemployment through the new Employment Zones.

Young unemployed people

9   For young people, entering the labour market is a critical rite of passage to adulthood. One of the factors causing social exclusion is an unacceptably high level of youth unemployment. The **New Deal for Young People** is a radical step forward because it emphasises quality, choice and above all meeting the needs of individuals. It will address all the barriers to work that young people face, including homelessness and drug dependency. It aims to help young unemployed people, aged 18 to 24, to find jobs and remain in employment. In the Budget, the Chancellor also announced that partners of young unemployed people who have no children would be included in the New Deal, and given access to the same opportunities for work.

The New Deal for Young People

- **Is being piloted in 12 pathfinder areas.**
- **Will go nationwide in April 1998.**
- **Is an investment of £2.6 billion.**

The New Deal for Young People *continued*

- Will offer participants, aged 18 to 24, four opportunities:
  - work with an employer who will receive a job subsidy of up to £60 a week;
  - full-time education or training;
  - work with a voluntary sector organisation; or
  - work on the Environmental Taskforce.

  All these options involve training.

- Support will also be given to those young people who see self-employment as the best route out of benefit dependency.

- Includes a special £750 grant to employers to provide their New Deal employees with training towards a recognised qualification.

- For those who do not wish to take up offers of help there will be no 'fifth option' of simply remaining on benefit.

10 Every young person who receives Jobseeker's Allowance (JSA) for six months without securing work will enter the New Deal Gateway – an exercise in promoting job-readiness and providing a tailor-made package of help. People with particular disadvantages may enter earlier. For those with adequate skills and appropriate work experience – the 'job-ready' – the immediate focus will be on securing an unsubsidised job. For those young people less equipped to enter the job market, the Gateway will provide careers advice and guidance, assessment of training needs, work trials with employers and tasters of other options. This Gateway period may last for up to four months.

Long-term unemployed people

11 For those who lack skills and become unemployed, the risks of remaining out of work for a long period are high. So prevention is better than cure. The Government's plans for lifelong learning, described in **Chapter Five**, are designed to raise skills in the adult population and promote employability, so that people find it easier to get and keep jobs.

12 There is already a sizeable group of long-term unemployed people who may need additional help to overcome barriers to work. Employers are often sceptical of the job-readiness of a person who has been out of the labour market for long periods. And, over time, skills, confidence and health can deteriorate. The **New Deal for the Long-Term Unemployed** represents the first serious attack on the waste of talents and resources represented by long-term unemployment.

> ### The New Deal for the Long-Term Unemployed
>
> - Due to start in June 1998.
>
> - Initial investment of £350 million.
>
> - For those aged over 25 who have been out of work for more than two years.
>
> - Substantial job subsidy of £75 a week for employers for six months.
>
> - Changes to benefit rules to improve access to full-time education or training.
>
>   *Additional pilots are due to start in November 1998:*
>
>   - Pilots of an intensive approach for 70,000 people, providing individualised advice, counselling and help, which may include training and work experience, at a cost of £100 million.
>
>   - Special assistance tailored to the needs of those aged over 50.

Lone Parents

13 The twin challenges of raising children alone and holding down a job are considerable. The vast majority of single parents want to work, to gain a decent wage and a foothold on the ladder out of poverty. But the old welfare system did little to help, simply handing out benefits rather than offering active support in finding and securing work, training or childcare. The **New Deal for Lone Parents** will provide a more active service.

> ### The New Deal for Lone Parents
>
> - Piloted in eight areas since July 1997, offering help to 40,000 lone parent households.
>
> - Available nationwide to lone parents making a new or repeat claim for Income Support from April 1998.
>
> - Available to all lone parents on Income Support from October 1998.
>
> - The service is aimed at lone parents whose youngest child is at school, but is also available to those with pre-school children.

14 There will be a full, independent evaluation of the first phase of the New Deal for Lone Parents, available in autumn 1999. Early indications are encouraging. Lone parent organisations, employers and lone parents themselves have all welcomed this New Deal, and the staff responsible for delivering the service have

been particularly enthusiastic. The staff have welcomed the opportunity to become involved in providing practical help and advice. The first phase of this New Deal has aroused considerable interest: lone parents in other parts of the country are asking if they can join in.

People with a disability or long-term illness

15 People with a disability or long-term illness are another group that often face difficulties in finding or remaining in work. Of course, many people with a disability or long-term illness are simply not in a position to undertake work. Our commitment to their welfare is unwavering. But there are others who may be able to work and who should get more help to do so. The **New Deal for Disabled People** has been introduced for this purpose. It is described in detail in **Chapter Six**.

Partners of the unemployed

16 The partner of an unemployed person can face additional disincentives to work: some people feel forced to give up their job once a partner becomes unemployed to avoid being made worse off. This is one cause of the deepening divide between *work-rich* and *work-poor* households. The partners of unemployed people are not offered the same assistance by the Government that is extended to the claimant unemployed. There are workless households in which the claimant (usually a man) is required to seek work actively, while the partner (usually a woman) is offered no help because of her assumed dependency.

17 We have therefore launched the **New Deal for Partners of the Unemployed.** As announced in the Budget, we have set aside £60 million of Windfall Tax receipts to provide partners with expert, personalised help to find work, through pilot projects in every region of the UK. Thousands of people – the vast majority of whom are women – will be helped by this expansion of the New Deal programme. In addition, we are expanding the New Deal for Young People to include partners of the young unemployed (see above).

Employment Zones

18 Alongside the New Deal, we are targeting intensive and innovative help on areas in particularly acute need. As our manifesto made clear, we are committed to finding ways of bringing together money currently spent separately on benefit, training and other programmes to be used more flexibly and innovatively in certain areas of the country, designated as **Employment Zones.** Local partnerships will draw up plans to give unemployed people opportunities to improve their employability and move back into and remain in employment.

19 Within existing legislation, we are already testing the approach in five prototype Employment Zones in Glasgow, South Teesside, Liverpool, North West Wales and Plymouth. £58 million has been provided to run these prototypes until the year 2000. We are considering how best to build fully-fledged Employment Zones on the experience of the prototypes from 2000.

20 At the same time, we are introducing a **New Deal for Communities** putting employment at the forefront of the drive against social exclusion. Further details are in **Chapter Eight**.

Flexible personalised service

21 The New Deal programme highlights the need for a new approach to service delivery. We are looking at the scope for moving towards a single work-focused gateway into the benefit system for all those of working age, providing customers with a **flexible, professional, personalised service**. In particular, we want to see whether more benefit claimants can be provided with a personal adviser who would help them develop a tailor-made action plan. This might involve:

- **identifying benefit needs;**

- **making an individual assessment of capacity for work;**

- **identifying barriers to labour market participation;**

- **offering help and advice in relation to jobsearch; and**

- **arranging mentoring support from older people with greater experience of the workplace.**

22 Evidence from a range of Employment Service programmes and the New Deal for Lone Parents, as well as similar projects in other countries, suggests that a service provided by personal advisers is valued by claimants and staff alike.

23 However, pilots are needed before the new approach is made available more generally. These will help establish the framework within which personal advisers will work and will assess what claimants can reasonably be asked to do and how to get the best value for money from the additional resources that the New Deal would require. We will link these pilots, wherever practicable, to related welfare-to-work initiatives, most notably Employment Zones, in order to provide the most effective packages of help to individuals to improve their employability and gain work.

Tackling barriers to work

24 The New Deals are designed to provide tailor-made help to individuals. But a number of other barriers to work also need to be addressed. Many of the tools for doing so are discussed in later chapters, including childcare and family-friendly employment (**Chapter Seven**) and education and health (**Chapter Five**). Other obstacles to work include the specific problems faced by sick and disabled people as well as lone parents.

25 Problems of employer perception also affect particular groups in society, especially **disabled people.** There is still a reluctance among some employers to take on or retain disabled employees. Equally, physical access to the workplace can cause difficulties. These sorts of problems are addressed by our proposals to strengthen anti-discrimination legislation, as described in **Chapter Six.**

26 **Lone parents** are another group who face particular barriers to work. The New Deal for Lone Parents addresses some of the key concerns, and our plans to help with childcare costs are described in **Chapter Seven.** But for many lone parents, the risk of leaving benefits can seem great, especially when the job may not be very secure or long-term. The Chancellor announced in the Budget a measure to help reduce the fears associated with swapping the certainty of benefits for the uncertainty of work. Lone parents who leave benefit and enter the workforce will have their entitlement to benefits protected – at the same rate – for 12 weeks.

Making work pay

Working Families Tax Credit

27 People who move from benefits to work, often overcoming significant barriers to do so, should be financially better-off as a result. Work should pay. The workings of the tax and benefit systems are crucial. The sharp withdrawal of means-tested benefits as wages come into the household can be a strong disincentive to work.

28 The proposed **Working Families Tax Credit (WFTC),** which will replace Family Credit from October 1999, will offer more generous support to working families with children and, by linking support more closely to the pay packet, will demonstrate the rewards of work as well as removing the stigma that is sometimes associated with claiming benefit. More generous provision towards childcare costs will be made, with a **Childcare Tax Credit** covering 70 per cent of childcare costs for low and middle income families (see **Chapter Seven**). Couples receiving WFTC will be able to choose whether the credit is paid to the mother or the father. No one will be forced to transfer money from 'purse to wallet', that is from women to men.

29 Most importantly, WFTC will boost the incomes of households moving into paid work and up the pay ladder. WFTC will be withdrawn at a rate of 55 per cent of net income, compared to 70 per cent in Family Credit. And, it will end marginal taxation rates in excess of 100 per cent for employees and reduce the number of families facing marginal rates of over 70 per cent by two-thirds.

30 Working families earning up to a net £90 a week will remain eligible for the maximum amount of WFTC, up from £77 a week in Family Credit. WFTC will mean that every working family with a full-time worker has an income of at least £180 a week.

Modernising National Insurance

31 As part of the Government's drive to promote work and cut red tape, we have decided to modernise National Insurance contributions. Our aims are two-fold: to increase the incentives for employers to take on staff, and to make work pay for all employees. From April 1999, we will:

- **align the starting point for employers' contributions with the single person's allowance for income tax (£81 a week from April), increasing by over 25 per cent the level of earnings at which employers start to pay National Insurance contributions, boosting incentives to hire;**

- **simplify employers' contributions and replace the array of four separate rates with a single employers' contribution rate of 12.2 per cent;**

- **abolish the 2 per cent entry fee currently paid by all employees who contribute. Future reforms will align the lower earnings limit (£64 a week from April) with the single person's tax allowance for income tax, ensuring that no one pays National Insurance for the first £81 of their weekly earnings and that all employees earning between £64 and £81 would have their rights to benefits protected; and**

- **examine the recommendations of Martin Taylor for reforming the National Insurance scheme as it applies to self-employed people.**

32 The Contributions Agency is to transfer from the Department of Social Security to the Inland Revenue in April 1999. This will reduce burdens on businesses who will only have to deal with one organisation for tax and National Insurance purposes.

33 Changes to the National Insurance scheme provide an opportunity to update the contributory principle. We will examine the link between paying contributions and earning entitlement to benefits with a view both to simplifying further adminstration of the scheme for employers and emphasising the link between work and earning benefit entitlement.

Income tax

34 The Government will introduce a **10p rate of income tax** when it is right for the economy to do so. Together with the new WFTC, this will lower the marginal rates of tax faced by those at the bottom of the labour market, where most people leaving benefits enter the world of work. This will create a fairer tax system and reduce the tax burden on lower-paid employment.

National minimum wage

35 Tax and benefit reforms form one half of our plans to make work pay. To accompany this we must also put in place measures to tackle low pay. The Government has introduced legislation to implement a **national minimum wage**, tackle exploitation and promote greater fairness in the workplace.

36 The level and coverage of the minimum wage will be decided by the Government, after considering the evidence from the Low Pay Commission. The Government's commitment to a floor under wages is unequivocal. Low pay raises the hurdles between benefit and wages: the national minimum wage will give a further boost to work incentives.

37 Ensuring that work makes people financially better off is crucial, but it is also important to keep in mind the non-financial benefits of work. Those in work enjoy better health than those on benefit. Work provides people with social networks and a sense of purpose. Even relatively low-paid jobs provide stepping stones to better-paid employment.

Responsibilities and rights

38 The responsibilities of individuals who can provide for themselves and their families to do so must always be matched by a responsibility on the part of government to provide opportunities for self-advancement. The Government's aim is to deliver services of such high quality that there would be simply no reason why people should not take them up.

39 The Government's commitment to expand significantly the range of help available therefore alters the contract with those who are capable of work. It is the Government's responsibility to promote work opportunities and to help people take advantage of them. It is the responsibility of those who can take them up to do so.

40 For example, the New Deal for Young People provides high quality options, all of which include education and training, designed to attain accredited qualifications. Those who unreasonably refuse an offer or fail to take up a place will be sanctioned.

Success Measures

1. **A reduction in the proportion of working age people living in workless households.**
2. **A reduction in the proportion of working age people out of work for more than two years.**
3. **An increase in the number of working age people in work.**
4. **An increase in the proportion of lone parents, people with a long-term illness and disabled people of working age in touch with the labour market.**

Chapter Four

New partnerships for welfare

> **Principle Two**
>
> The public and private sectors should work in partnership to ensure that, wherever possible, people are insured against foreseeable risks and make provision for their retirement.

1. When William Beveridge, the architect of the post-war welfare state, began his working life, one of his first priorities was to examine the root causes of poverty amid relative plenty – and how to prevent it. This quest remains vital. But it is equally important today to examine why so many people are comfortably off – and how to replicate their success. For most people of working age, secure, well-paid work is paramount, as **Chapter Three** discussed. But for others, especially pensioners, the key to rising prosperity has been the rapid growth of private-public partnerships for saving. Occupational pensions are the clearest example, and are arguably the biggest welfare success story of the century.

2. Private-public partnerships have developed in other areas too.

- *Family bereavement:* survivors' benefits are provided mainly by the private sector. Most private pension schemes provide survivors' benefits and indeed are obliged to if they are formally 'contracted out' of the State Earnings Related Pension Scheme (SERPS). In 1995 the private sector paid out £2 billion in life policies. The Government has a smaller – but still substantial role. Each year it pays out about £1 billion in widows' benefits, and State Retirement Pensions provide further survivors' benefits.

- *Industrial injuries:* Employers are required to insure against the risk of work injuries for which they are at fault. In 1995 they paid out £738 million in compensation and costs. The Government compensates workers – through Industrial Injuries Benefits – for injuries and for certain industrial diseases. Last year these benefits amounted to £730 million.

3. In addition, the provision of income during short-term sickness is now largely the responsibility of employers – nine out of ten employees are covered by some form of occupational sick pay. This occupational provision is matched by government provision for long-term sickness through Incapacity Benefit, which costs about £7.8 billion.

4   The UK needs more welfare, not less. With an ageing population and rising expectations, the growth of partnerships is good news. However, the following key problems remain:

- **large numbers of people still cannot join good occupational pension schemes and are not benefiting from the improved provision for retirement;**

- **provision for a number of contingencies is currently insufficient, including long-term care and protection for homebuyers against the loss of income; and**

- **greater non-government provision highlights the importance of good regulation. The misselling of personal pensions was an example that demonstrated how easy it can be both to erode public support and to breed insecurity.**

5   We therefore aim to expand provision by:

- **ensuring that today's and tomorrow's pensioners have a decent income in retirement;**

- **getting help to the poorest pensioners;**

- **providing fair and effective mechanisms for funding long-term care;**

- **encouraging savings through Individual Savings Accounts;**

- **ensuring better protection for homebuyers;**

- **ensuring that people are not discouraged from making private provision; and**

- **making sure financial services are properly regulated.**

■ POLICY DIRECTION

Ensuring that all pensioners have a decent income in retirement

6   Pensions are the most developed and successful example of a public-private partnership. It is thanks in large part to the growth of occupational pensions that many pensioners are now able to enjoy a comfortable retirement.

7   Today, three-quarters of workers have a private pension. Eleven million employees belong to their company scheme – 4.5 million more than in 1953. At least another 8 million people – employees and self-employed – hold a personal pension, four times as many as did a mere ten years ago. The value of funds invested in occupational and personal pensions exceeds £800 billion. These pensions are now paying out £30 billion a year. In addition, the state spends annually:

- **£30 billion a year on the basic State Retirement Pension;**

- **£13 billion in tax relief on pension contributions;**

- **£7 billion in National Insurance reliefs for people who opt-out of SERPS in favour of a private alternative;**

- **£17 billion on SERPS plus means-tested and disability benefits for pensioners.**

8   This public-private partnership is built up in a series of tiers.

- **The first-tier is provided by the Government through the universal basic State Retirement Pension and is funded through workers' National Insurance contributions on a pay-as-you-go basis.**

- **The second-tier is mostly provided privately through company schemes and personal pensions, though SERPS provides a public option. Nearly everyone in work is compelled to have a second-tier pension. All 19 million employees who earn more than the lower earnings limit for National Insurance (£64 a week from April 1998), and their employers, are required to pay some of that National Insurance into a private pension or SERPS. The self-employed are exempt from this compulsory second-tier.**

- **The third-tier is voluntary private provision in excess of the compulsory minimum. Perhaps 14 million workers - including half the self-employed - have such provision. Inland Revenue rules give tax relief on contributions within certain limits.**

9   Alongside these tiers are means-tested benefits provided by the Government. These are designed to ensure that no one lives on less than Income Support of £70 a week for single people, £109 a week for couples, after rent and council tax bills have been paid. At least 3.3 million pensioners receive help through this route. A further one million pensioners fail to claim the Income Support they are due.

10 The box below shows how the balance of state and private support differs for people on different incomes.

> ### Some examples of pension provision
>
> A care assistant earning £8,000 a year and making no private pension provision, pays National Insurance (NI) contributions and builds up rights to State Retirement Pension, both basic and SERPS. She receives no tax relief on pension contributions, nor NI rebates. If her earnings remained constant in real terms for a full working life, she would receive a total State Retirement Pension of £4,550 for each year in retirement.
>
> A security guard earning £15,000 a year has a contracted-out personal pension. He pays NI contributions, and builds up rights to basic State Retirement Pension, but a rebate of part of his NI contributions (both his and his employer's) is paid into his personal pension fund. He makes no additional pension contributions. He receives £60 a year in tax relief and £530 a year in NI rebates, assuming he is aged 35, giving a combined total of tax relief and rebates of £590 a year. If these earnings and contributions continued for the whole of his working life, his total pension would be £7,040 a year, just under half being from the basic State Retirement Pension and the rest from his personal pension.
>
> A finance director earning £50,000 a year and a member of a contracted-out salary-related occupational pension scheme, pays NI contributions and builds up rights to the basic State Retirement Pension. A rebate of part of her NI contributions, plus additional employer and employee contributions (the latter equal to 5 per cent of her earnings), are paid into the occupational pension fund. She receives £1,670 a year in tax relief and £960 a year in NI rebates, giving a combined total of tax relief and rebates of £2,630 a year. If she had a full working life, and her final salary was £50,000 a year, she would get on retirement a tax free lump sum of £75,000 and a total pension of £28,250 a year, most of which wouldbe from the occupational scheme.

11 The flourishing public-private partnership has delivered a substantial increase in average living standards for pensioners. The average income of a pensioner today is over 60 per cent higher in real terms than in 1979. This is almost half as much again as the growth in incomes of the rest of the population. Of the increase 37 per cent has come from occupational pensions, 25 per cent from other savings (including personal pensions) and 34 per cent from the Government.

12 But the partnership has failed to deliver a decent standard of living for all pensioners. The incomes of the poorest 20 per cent of single pensioners have risen by only 30 per cent in real terms, compared with an increase of over 70 per cent for the richest 20 per cent. More worryingly, the poorest pensioners receive modest incomes – just £70 a week net income for the poorest fifth of single pensioners in 1995/96 – and even the median for all single pensioners is only £105 a week.

13   The Government is pledged to retain the basic State Retirement Pension as the foundation of pension provision. However, the problem of the poorest pensioners exposes four key weaknesses in the second-tier of the public–private partnership:

- personal pensions currently on offer can be a bad deal for people on low or intermittent pay;

- the need to strengthen the regulation of personal pensions, where misselling has knocked public confidence;

- there is no provision for carers who are outside the labour market; and

- some people are failing to save enough or failing to save at all, especially given:

    – rising expectations about how much income is needed for a comfortable retirement; and

    – the fact that retirement itself is getting longer as life expectancy increases.

14   A **Green Paper on pensions** later this year will set out specific proposals for addressing the weaknesses highlighted above. Here we set out our current thinking:

- In place of poor value private pensions, we will introduce low cost Stakeholder Pension schemes which will give low paid workers the chance to save for a decent private second pension. Stakeholder Pensions will be required to meet minimum standards to ensure they are good value for money. To keep costs low they will be collective schemes, and could be delivered by mutual organisations, including trade unions.

- Regulation – the new Financial Services Authority (FSA) will establish and enforce high standards for the regulation of investments including personal pensions.

- There is presently no cover for carers. We are examining the creation of a Citizenship Pension.

- Low savings – many submissions to the Pensions Review have argued that the compulsory second-tier, which already covers three quarters of the work force, should be extended to groups not covered and that the minimum second-tier contributions should be raised from the current National Insurance rebate levels. We are looking at these proposals seriously.

15 The Green Paper on pensions will report the findings of the Pensions Review, which has been considering all aspects of state and private provision, including the basic State Retirement Pension.

16 Separately, the Government will be consulting on draft legislation for **pension sharing on divorce**, during the current parliamentary session.

Helping the poorest pensioners

17 We are committed to getting more automatic help to the poorest pensioners. As a first step, we have already provided extra help to all pensioners over the winter.

18 One million pensioners fail to take up Income Support, losing on average £16 per week, and we want to get help to them fast. There seem to be a number of barriers stopping these pensioners from claiming their benefit entitlement, and we are determined that they will be removed. We have commissioned research into why they fail to claim.

19 In addition, we will be running a number of pilot exercises to test the most effective ways of identifying and reaching these pensioners and preventing problems of low take-up among pensioners in future. The pilots involve the Benefits Agency, local authorities and local voluntary groups and will involve greater use of information technology and electronically produced forms. Pensioner-friendly means of contact will minimise problems of complexity and stigma.

20 Together, the research and the pilot exercises will equip us to find the best possible way of delivering the extra help to which these pensioners are already entitled, and to overcome the barriers which are stopping them from enjoying a higher standard of living.

21 The Government's measures to help all pensioners are outlined in the box below.

Government action for pensioners

- We have kept our promise to retain the basic State Retirement Pension and to increase it at least in line with prices.

- We have taken action for better and cheaper insulation, and to cut fuel bills further by reducing VAT on domestic fuels to 5 per cent.

- We have committed £400 million to help pensioners pay their fuel bills for last winter and for next. Pensioner households are entitled to £20, and the poorest pensioner households receive more – £50.

- We have announced plans for a series of pilots to look at ways of helping pensioners to take up the Income Support to which they are entitled.

Government action for pensioners *continued*

- **We have set up a Royal Commission to advise us on the funding of long-term care.**

- **We are cutting red tape in the health service and spending more on patients – who are drawn disproportionately from the elderly population. Over this year and next, the Government has allocated an extra £2 billion for the NHS.**

- **Our Crime and Disorder Bill deals with the unacceptable behaviour which makes life a misery for many pensioners and should make communities safer places for all to enjoy.**

Providing fair and effective mechanisms for funding long-term care

22 The 'greying' of society has policy implications beyond pensions, most importantly for the provision of long-term care. The Government recognises that pensioners are concerned, not only to have a decent income in retirement, but also to receive good-quality care should they be unable to look after themselves. The majority of those needing long-term care are aged over 75. The increase in the numbers of elderly people in the population is therefore likely to lead to an increase in the numbers needing care.

23 Between 1996 and 2031, the number of people aged 65 and over is projected to grow by about 55 per cent and the number aged 85 and over by around 75 per cent. However, a number of other factors also need to be considered when assessing the effect of demography on the demand for long-term care, in particular the nature and extent of future medical advances, the extent of informal care and future changes to the real costs of care.

24 There are long-term care products on the market, but the private market is not well developed, in part because of difficulties in assessing the risks of future care needs. Private provision carries with it the risk of the market 'cherry picking' of the best risks, leaving the taxpayer to pick up the tab for the rest. The Government has established a **Royal Commission** to devise proposals for a sustainable system of funding long-term care provision in both the short and the long-term. The Commission is due to report by early next year.

Encouraging savings by Individual Savings Accounts

25 The Government is committed to encouraging savings by all. As announced in the Budget, **Individual Savings Accounts** will start in April 1999 and will be available for at least ten years, subject to review after seven years. These accounts will include cash, National Savings, shares and life insurance. Savers will be able to subscribe up to £5,000 a year (£7,000 in 1999/2000) to these accounts. The accounts will be subject neither to income tax nor to capital gains tax, and there will be a 10 per cent tax credit on cash dividends from shares invested in the new accounts for the first five years of their operation.

26 We particularly want to encourage greater saving by those on lower incomes. The new accounts will be accessible, flexible savings mechanisms, with no tax penalties for withdrawing savings and no minimum subscription. Our research has indicated that the new savings accounts will appeal to those who have not saved before, as well as to those who have. They should therefore spread the savings habit to those on more modest incomes. The ten-year scheme will give savers the stability to take a long-term view and to build up savings for their future. Those savings will dovetail with pension savings for retirement.

Better protection for home-buyers

27 Another area where closer partnership between the Government and the financial services industry could be fruitful is the provision of protection for those home-buyers who run into difficulty paying their mortgage. Home owners are not well-protected at present. Help through the benefit system (Income Support Mortgage Interest [ISMI]) is confined to people receiving Income Support or income-based Jobseeker's Allowance; most claimants wait for nine months before ISMI is paid; and many do not have insurance.

28 Currently, mortgage payment protection policies provide too narrow a range of cover, for too short a period, and are taken out by too few people. The Council of Mortgage Lenders and the Association of British Insurers are working with their members on better products for owner-occupiers, and the Government is an active partner in this process, helping to encourage greater provision outside the orbit of government.

Ensuring that people are not discouraged from making private provision

29 A good example of how private provision can be discouraged by the benefit system is creditor insurance – insurance for loan repayments against loss of income. Currently, creditor insurance can be discouraged by the benefit system, since Jobseeker's Allowance and Income Support can be reduced by the full amount of insurance payments made directly to claimants. By contrast, creditor insurance payments made direct to creditors do not normally affect income-related benefits.

30 Following consultation with the insurance and banking industries, the Government proposes to change the law. We will be laying regulations, subject to statutory consultation, to ensure that income-related benefits are not cut because of income from creditor insurance, irrespective of the payment methods, so long as such income is intended and used to cover past debt.

Regulation of financial services

31 Private-public partnerships highlight the need for regulation of financial services, with government providing an effective and reliable regulatory environment. Extended funded pension coverage will be a flagship model for this approach.

32 The regulatory process should provide reassurance and protection for customers, without imposing excessive costs, which in the end can only diminish the value customers get. The Government looks to the new FSA to meet this important responsibility for investments such as personal pensions. The FSA will set, promote and enforce high standards of integrity and competence in order to protect customers and secure fair treatment. One of the FSA's statutory objectives will be to ensure that regulation is cost-effective.

33 The Government is also considering whether, in selected areas, there may be scope for encouraging product providers to develop simple, transparent products which customers can easily assess. The Government will shortly consult about setting voluntary benchmarks for Individual Savings Accounts to encourage product providers to market good-value savings products. These products should offer ease of access without penalty terms and should be attractive to new or inexperienced savers. Another option is to set entry conditions for Stakeholder Pensions designed to deliver simplicity and good value.

34 Non-government providers of welfare must also be allowed to compete fairly. We must ensure a fair playing field. The institutions of welfare which compete in the marketplace but are owned by the people they provide for – friendly societies and mutual organisations – have a crucial and growing role.

Success Measures

1. At the end of the process of reform, there should be a guarantee of a decent income in retirement for all.

2. An increase in the amount of money going towards savings and insurance, but without increasing the proportion borne by government.

3. An extension in high-quality second-tier pension provision to a greater proportion of the working population.

4. An increase in public confidence in the quality and regulation of private sector savings, pensions and insurance products.

Chapter Five

The importance of welfare services

Principle Three

The new welfare state should provide public services of high quality to the whole community, as well as cash benefits.

1. The welfare state is not simply the benefits system. A range of services – including education, health, job assistance, childcare and nursery education, transport, social services and housing – are at least as important both in lifting people out of poverty and providing opportunity.

2. But our public services are suffering from under-investment and old ways of working. Our commitment is investment for reform: new money but, in return, a new emphasis on standards, quality and efficiency. And again, the barriers between public and private provision should be broken down. What counts should be what works. This is evident in the recent transport proposals published for London. Later, more detailed plans for our transport system for the whole of Britain will be published. But reform is underway already in education, health and housing.

■ POLICY DIRECTION

Education and lifelong learning

3. Education and skills help individuals achieve security and mobility. A skilled workforce is also essential for our collective prosperity.

4. Given that rising returns to education and training explain a large part of the rise in wage inequality, raising educational standards and the provision of lifelong learning have key roles to play in creating a fairer, but flexible, labour market. Employment security increasingly depends not on attachment to a single employer, but on having skills that will attract a range of employers.

5. Learning begins at school – the starting point of our reform programme. We want further and higher education to become an expectation and opportunity for the many, not the few. Learning must become a lifetime activity.

6. The key challenges are to:

- **raise standards in education and training;**

- **widen access to further and higher education; and**

- **make a reality of lifelong learning.**

Raising standards in education and training

7   The Government has set out a comprehensive programme of measures to improve schools in England in the White Paper, *Excellence in Schools*. We will work in partnership with all those committed to raising standards in education, to give every child and young person a firm foundation for the future. At the school level, too many pupils still fail to achieve their potential. Too many leave school with few qualifications. And too many who have left compulsory education never return to learning. The differences in performance between schools and groups of pupils are unacceptable. There will be zero tolerance of under-performance in schools. We have made it clear that we want success for everyone and will apply consistent pressure for improvements matched by steady support for those who need it to achieve higher standards.

8   The Government's programme of school reforms is based on a range of strategies to improve educational standards. These include:

- **expanding pre-school education;**

- **campaigning to improve literacy and numeracy in primary education, to ensure that children have the tools for learning;**

- **reducing class sizes in infant schools;**

- **introducing Education Action Zones, which will provide support and development in the areas where they are most needed;**

- **promoting setting, so that the comprehensive system is updated for today's world;**

- **ensuring autonomy for all schools over how they are managed; and**

- **establishing after-school clubs to enhance children's opportunities to learn, particularly those children at greatest risk of under-achieving. The Government has already set aside £200 million to help build up out-of-school hours learning activities.**

9   The Scottish Office is also focusing on raising standards in schools. Among the actions it has taken is the introduction of an early intervention programme to assist early reading and a programme of pilot schemes to develop innovative alternatives to exclusion from school. It has also set out a framework for the setting of targets for improvements in all schools in Scotland.

10 Improvements at school level will enhance opportunities for young people to pursue their learning beyond compulsory education, in further and higher education. The Government has made a commitment to half a million extra places in further and higher education.

Widening access to higher education

11   Higher education is an investment in society's future. We are committed to maintaining and improving quality in higher education, as well as to widening access. At present, at least a quarter of adults undertake no learning at all after leaving school. We want wider participation in higher education, especially by those from semi-skilled and unskilled family backgrounds, or from disadvantaged areas, as well as people with disabilities, all currently under-represented in higher education.

12   The investment by the nation in education must be balanced by commitment from individuals. On average, graduates earn more and have more secure jobs than non-graduates. The Government therefore believes that they should share the cost. The **new funding arrangement**s for higher education are based on the principle that costs should be shared between the taxpayer and those who reap the biggest financial rewards from degree level study. But important safeguards will be put in place to ensure fairness. There will be no tuition fees for full-time undergraduate students from lower income families; there will be no increase in parental contributions. Students will be helped with living costs if necessary. Repayments after graduation will be managed more fairly than under the current scheme.

13   These new funding arrangements will mean more money for universities and will allow us to lift the cap on student numbers. The Government will ensure that savings are used to improve quality, standards and opportunities for all in higher education.

Widening access to further education

14   *The Learning Age,* the Government's lifelong learning consultation paper, was published alongside detailed responses to the Kennedy report on widening participation in further education. The further education sector is diverse and has developed a capacity to generate important social and economic benefits through lifelong learning opportunities. It caters for around four million students in England alone, 80 per cent of them adult, studying for some 17,000 different qualifications. Further education provision has expanded by over a quarter in the last four years.

15   The Government has strong expectations that colleges should continue to provide many fresh, high quality opportunities – particularly for those who have not achieved their full potential in the past – and has therefore set out a framework for continuing high standards in further education. We want to see annual targets to improve retention and achievement; improvements in college management; and better teaching in further education, building on the best of current practice. A new **National Training Organisation** in further education will help to secure this.

16   We are also reviewing the current arrangements for financial support for students in further education, including adults, with a view to establishing a coherent system which is simpler, more equitable and better targeted on those most in need.

Making a reality of lifelong learning

17 Learning does not stop at the school, or even university, gates. The Government's vision is of a learning society in which everyone has opportunities to improve their knowledge and skills throughout their lives. Realising this vision will require a major change in culture, a sustained revolution in aspiration and achievement, and a continuing collective effort by individuals, employers and the Government. The proposed **University for Industry** will be designed to open up access to learning to many for whom it has been unattainable in the past. And proposed **Individual Learning Accounts** will help make a reality of those opportunities. As a first step, we propose to support up to a million learning accounts, with a public contribution of £150 for each account.

18 Community, adult and family learning have vital parts to play in lifelong learning. In *The Learning Age,* we launched a new **Adult and Community Learning Fund** to sustain and encourage new schemes to improve access to learning alongside other measures to strengthen basic skills crucial to modern life.

Health and social services

19 The National Health Service (NHS) has always been a core and cherished element of the post-war welfare state. In the 50 years since its foundation, the NHS has overcome many challenges. As the war against infectious diseases, such as smallpox and polio, has been won, other threats to life and health have grown, notably cancer, heart disease and new infectious diseases, such as HIV/AIDS. Rapidly-developing medical and scientific advances have improved the ability of doctors, nurses and other health care professionals to diagnose and treat illness. We have learnt a good deal about what we can do to stay healthy. But the NHS faces a number of challenges.

20 First, the NHS needs reform and modernisation. The health service remains focused on the treatment of illness rather than its prevention, and the current internal market encourages the *status quo*. Secondly, the benefits of the service are not shared equally. While the health of the population is increasing overall, the health of the best-off is improving faster than the health of the worst-off. Above all, those in greatest need – among them people suffering multiple deprivation, including large numbers from black and ethnic minority groups – often have the greatest difficulty in accessing good quality health services.

21 Inequalities in health mirror inequalities in income, job opportunities, living standards and education. Policies to combat social exclusion, boost jobs and skills are crucial to narrowing the health divide. We will move towards a more preventive health system and ensure better access to services.

Better services, better access

22 We have signalled our intention to abolish the old internal market in the health service and replace it with a framework based on co-operation. However, to help the efficiency drive, there is also a range of new performance indicators, changes in practice, reorganisation of primary care, and a focus on clinical standards and excellence. Money freed up by reducing bureaucracy, together with a substantial additional cash investment in the NHS, will go to improve front-line services, both in hospitals and the community.

23 We are determined to improve access to health services – preventative and reactive – for those most in need. If you are ill or injured, there will be an NHS to help, regardless of ability to pay, who your GP happens to be, or where you live. This principle of equal access is reflected in a new *NHS National Performance Framework*. For example, local services will be monitored to ensure that black and ethnic minority groups are not disadvantaged in terms of access to local health services.

24 The Government are also establishing a number of **Health Action Zones** with a further wave to follow in 1999. They will work for more effective services and demonstrable improvements in the health of the population, with a strong emphasis on community involvement and partnership.

25 For the most vulnerable in society, social services are often as important as health care. In particular, they make an enormous contribution to the well-being of individuals, communities and society, by:

- **providing for older people, whether at home or in residential care;**

- **protecting and caring for vulnerable children and young people in such a way as to improve their life chances;**

- **supporting people with mental health problems; and**

- **helping people with disabilities to live as independently as possible.**

26 In addition, the Government will publish a White Paper later this year, setting out how social services can be made more responsive to the needs of those who use them.

A new emphasis on prevention

27 The Government's agenda for health moves beyond a reactive approach to illness and sets out a bold vision for a health service with a clearer focus on promoting good health disease prevention. Our key aims are: to improve the health of the population as a whole, by increasing the length of people's lives and the number of years people spend free from illness; as well as narrowing the health gap.

28 To meet our goals we have set out a national contract for better health which sets out the action needed – from government, local organisations and from individuals – to make real improvements in health. The strategy for England sets four national targets on heart disease and strokes, cancers, accidents and mental health. Similar strategies are being developed for the rest of the UK. In Scotland, a strategy for a concerted inter-sectoral approach to health improvement has been developed, with a particular focus on tackling health inequalities. At district level,

Health Authorities will draw up **Health Improvement Programmes** setting out comprehensive local strategies for improving the health of the communities they serve.

29   At a local level, the Government is providing local communities with the means to play their part in the health strategy, using £300 million from the National Lottery. A network of **Healthy Living Centres** will be set up across the country. These flagships for health in the community will be particularly important in the most deprived areas, and for those people in poorest health or who find existing health and fitness facilities off-putting or inaccessible.

30   Sir Donald Acheson, former Chief Medical Officer, is to report back on the main trends in health inequalities, to identify the areas of policy which evidence suggests are likely to offer opportunities for Government to develop beneficial, cost effective and affordable interventions to reduce inequalities.

Housing

31   Help with rent through Housing Benefit and support to local authorities and housing associations, will remain an important element of support for people who are retired, in low-paid work, or who are temporarily or permanently unable to take-up work. This support is designed to help these groups afford reasonable accommodation. There are links between suitable, decent housing and good health and indications that decent housing can have positive effects in other areas too, such as educational attainment.

32   There are concentrations of unfit and dilapidated housing in the areas of greatest deprivation – communities with high rates of unemployment and crime, poor facilities, vandalism and other problems. Physically-decaying, poor housing is a characteristic of marginalised communities. The unemployed and the vulnerable become trapped in such areas, while residents who are able to exercise choice move away. The Government has released capital receipts to break the back-log of housing repairs and reduce homelessness by tackling unmet housing need. The Rough Sleepers Initiative has been expanded to 27 cities beyond the streets of London. Reducing rough sleeping is one of the core aims of the Social Exclusion Unit which will report later this year. Tackling the problems of the most deprived estates and localities is another of the Unit's core aims. The Best Value regime will encourage all local authorities to provide the highest quality of housing management and services to their tenants and residents.

33   In the last 20 years, there has been a substantial shift in the way government supports rented housing, away from 'bricks and mortar' subsidies to personal subsidies through Housing Benefit. In 1979, in England alone, the Government spent £11 billion (1996/97 prices) subsidising 'bricks and mortar' and about £2 billion on Housing Benefit. Today, those figures are virtually reversed: Housing Benefit costs £11 billion – around 12.5 per cent of the social security budget – and 'bricks and mortar' spending has shrunk to under £3 billion.

- 4.7 million people now claim Housing Benefit, 20 per cent more than in 1990/91;

- 40 per cent of claimants are pensioners, 19 per cent lone parents, 16 per cent unemployed and 14 per cent sick and disabled people; and

- 60 per cent of claimants are council house tenants, 23 per cent live in the private rented sector and 17 per cent in housing association property.

34 The shift in government support for rented housing over the last 20 years means that its help is now much more closely targeted on the poor. Housing Benefit has underpinned the growth in housing provided by housing associations, attracting nearly £12 billion in private finance, and has helped to finance an expansion of the private rented sector. It helps give people on low incomes security in their homes. But the growth has had disadvantages too:

- **Housing Benefit takes away responsibility from claimants. Tenants on benefit have little interest in the rent – provided it meets local limits, it can be reimbursed in full.**

- **Landlords can exploit Housing Benefit by aiming to set rents at the maximum benefit will pay.**

- **Housing Benefit can act as a deterrent to work: many tenants lose 65p of Housing Benefit for every extra £1 of income they bring in above the Income Support level. This high marginal tax rate faced by the low paid is magnified if they also receive Family Credit and Council Tax Benefit.**

- **High rents and more claimants mean more people are caught in a deeper benefit trap.**

- **Housing Benefit is complex, unpredictable, and inconsistently administered.**

- **An estimated £1 billion is lost in Housing Benefit fraud each year.**

35 Reforming housing and Housing Benefit policy raises many difficult questions, which have defeated successive governments in the past. In the immediate term, we are taking steps to tackle Housing Benefit fraud. The Working Families Tax Credit and other changes announced in the Budget will reduce the disincentive effects caused by the combination of Housing Benefit and Family Credit. For the longer term, the Government is reviewing the underlying relationship between housing policy and Housing Benefit, to address the weaknesses of the current regime. We aim to develop stable and sustainable policies, in line with the overall objectives of welfare reform, striking a better balance between tenants' rights and responsibilities.

Success Measures

1. An improvement in the health of the population as a whole by increasing the length of people's lives and the number of years they spend free from illness.

2. An increase in the proportion of 11 year-olds with good literacy and numeracy skills and a reduction in the number of school leavers with no recognised qualifications.

3. An increase in the proportion of the adult population with educational qualifications.

4. An improvement in the quality of housing and housing management.

Chapter Six

Support for disabled people

Principle Four

Those who are disabled should get the support they need to lead a fulfilling life with dignity.

1. Disabled people have a huge contribution to make to the nation. But too often they have been written off by a society which has failed to tackle discrimination; give those who want to work the help and rehabilitation they need; or ensure dignity and independence to those disabled people who cannot work.

Many people with a disability or long-term illness are simply not in a position to undertake work. Our commitment to their welfare is unwavering. The Government will work to ensure that they are not left on society's sidelines.

2. The new welfare state will give disabled people the opportunities denied them in the past so that they are able to live fulfilling and independent lives. We will:

- introduce effective civil rights for disabled people;

- remove the barriers to work and give active help to disabled people who wish to work;

- fundamentally reform Incapacity Benefit (IB) for future claimants; and

- ensure the welfare system recognises the extra costs faced by disabled people.

■ POLICY DIRECTION

Civil rights for disabled people

3   Ensuring the wider social participation of disabled people is a key goal for the Government. Disabled people want to be as independent as possible but too often society disables them. Civil rights are crucial to ensure disabled people have equal opportunities. The Government has a three-point strategy for introducing comprehensive and enforceable civil rights:

- **the Disability Rights Task Force – already established – which will recommend the best way forward in securing civil rights for disabled people;**

- **a Disability Rights Commission will be established to protect, enforce and promote the rights of disabled people; and**

- **the Disability Discrimination Act: we will implement the remaining provisions, bringing practical benefits for disabled people in their everyday lives.**

Help for disabled people who wish to work

The New Deal

4   Survey evidence shows that up to one million disabled people would like to return to work if they were given the right assistance. The New Deal is the first programme ever to provide disabled people who want to work with the opportunities to do so and the assistance they need. It marks a clean break with the past, when disabled people were left for years on benefit without help or advice on how to return to work and regain financial independence.

The New Deal for Disabled People

- **£195 million earmarked for this Parliament.**

- **Support for innovative schemes to test a range of ideas for helping people with a disability or long-term illness move into, or remain in, work.**

- **Funding for personal adviser pilots to co-ordinate help and support for disabled people and people with a long-term illness.**

5   The bidding process for **innovative schemes** is well under way. We have received more than 120 bids in the first round, and the first contracts are due to be awarded later in the spring. A second tranche of bids will be submitted in July, with further contracts awarded in the early autumn.

6   We are also embarking on a series of pilots to assess the effectiveness of **personal advisers**, offering individualised help to disabled people who want to move into work. Personal advisers will co-ordinate a range of services, including action planning, job preparation and job placement, and advice on benefits to help people with a disability or a long-term illness when they move into work. The first pilots will start in six areas in October 1998, with a further six areas added early in 1999. Customer-focused services should increase the number of people with a disability or long-term illness who are in touch with the labour market.

7   The pilots will supply more information on the difficulties faced by different groups of disabled people in relation to the labour market, and help us develop well-targeted strategies for overcoming them. For example, some people who have experienced mental illness face particular problems because of the fluctuating nature of their conditions and employers' reactions. We will consult widely on approaches to support people with mental illness who want to work and circulate examples of good employer practice to employment and support agencies.

Barriers to work

8   Disabled people face a series of barriers to work.

- The <u>unemployment trap</u>, which means disabled people are often worse off in work because of the loss of benefits. We are tackling the unemployment trap by providing more financial help to disabled people who find work. In the Budget, the Chancellor announced the introduction, from October 1999, of a new Disabled Person's Tax Credit to replace Disability Working Allowance. This new tax credit will provide more generous help and make more support available to more disabled people.

- The <u>limits on the amount of work</u> which disabled people can do without losing their benefit under present rules. Disabled people receiving benefits because they are considered unfit for work can do, at most, 16 hours a week of voluntary or therapeutic work without losing their benefit. In addition, the period of time during which disabled people can take up a job and return to benefit if their health fails is limited to eight weeks. We propose a number of changes, some for national implementation and some for piloting. At the national level, we intend – as announced in the Budget – to extend the period for which benefit rates are protected from eight weeks to one year, and to abolish the 16 hour restriction on unpaid voluntary work. The pilots we propose would include allowing people on IB to:

- retain benefits while undertaking work for trial periods;

- do a small amount of paid work, subject to a weekly limit of £15, without loss of benefit; and

- have access to Jobfinder's grants of £200 and, for the first six months of part-time work, to Jobmatch payments of £50 a week – both currently limited to unemployed people – to ease the transition into work.

- **Employer discrimination**: which we are tackling through implementing the Disability Discrimination Act and establishing the Disability Rights Commission.

Reforming Incapacity Benefit

9   From a relatively minor part of the benefit system 20 years ago, IB has grown to a cost of £7.8 billion – almost one tenth of the social security budget. Today 1.75 million people receive it – three times as many as in 1979. Over this period, IB has proved a simple, but costly escape route for government to keep the unemployment numbers down. In some cases IB has taken on the characteristics of a more generous form of unemployment benefit. That was never the intention. It is an insurance benefit for those incapable of working.

10   A key problem with IB is the All Work Test. It writes off as unfit for work people who might, with some assistance, be able to return to work, perhaps in a new occupation. It is an all or nothing test, in the sense that it assesses people as either fit for work or unfit for any work. Thus many people who would be capable of some work with the right help and rehabilitation are instead spending their working lives on benefit. We want a new approach to IB which focuses on what disabled people can do, not on what they cannot. While we will keep the current assessment system for existing claimants, we are examining the scope for a more effective test for future claimants which assesses the scale of their employability, recognising that capacity for work is a continuum. People with some capacity to work would then be given the opportunity of the assistance they need to help them return to work.

11   Over time, less money will be spent on IB as more people make a successful return to work and fewer people remain on benefit. Savings made can be used to support severely disabled people with the greatest needs.

Support for disabled people

12 Two important components of support for disabled people are Disability Living Allowance (DLA) and Attendance Allowance (AA), which help meet the extra costs of disability. We are committed to the principle of providing special allowances to help with these extra costs and we intend to maintain DLA and AA as universal, national benefits for those who meet the entitlement conditions.

13 However, there is a question about whether some people receiving these benefits are entitled to them and whether others who are entitled are not getting the help they need. In order to receive DLA and AA, disabled people make a statement of their care and mobility needs, usually backed up by evidence from a GP. Only in a minority of cases is the claimant asked to undergo an independent medical test.

14 The recent joint investigation of DLA by the DLA Advisory Board and the Department of Social Security suggested that in two-thirds of cases there was insufficient evidence to support the benefit claim. They also found that one-third of the awards made for life (two thirds of all awards) were made to people whose condition might have been expected to improve. On the other hand, early evidence from a forthcoming disability survey suggests present take-up of DLA may be as low as 40 per cent to 60 per cent.

15 We now want to undertake a review of the gateway to DLA and AA. We plan to set up a forum with organisations of and for disabled people to discuss how the benefits can be reformed to fix these problems.

16 The Benefits Integrity Project – which is designed to check the validity of DLA claims – is not working well. It has a series of structural flaws which we are dealing with one by one in consultation with disability organisations.

17 We realise that disabled people's concerns range wider than rights and benefits. Like all citizens, they are concerned with the whole range of government policies and services that affect them. We will be taking steps to ensure improved cross-departmental policy development and delivery affecting disabled people, their families and carers, and those providing services for them, in order to secure both better results and better value for money.

Success Measures

1. A reduction in discrimination against disabled people.

2. An increase in the number of disabled people able to work.

3. A reduction in spending on Incapacity Benefit as the number of claimants falls, with more resources available to help severely disabled people with the greatest needs.

4. A simpler, clearer and fairer system for determining entitlement to disability benefits.

Chapter Seven

Support for families and children

Principle Five

The system should support families and children, as well as tackling the scourge of child poverty.

1. A fundamental principle of the welfare state should be to support families and children. But the way of doing that today must change. The shape of the family has changed significantly in recent decades. But families remain the building block of society. Children thrive in a secure home with loving parents. The family unit provides adults and children alike with emotional and financial support. By pooling income, families ensure a higher quality of life for all their members. But there have been significant pressures on the family. Men and women struggle with balancing work and family responsibilities. In addition, there is a huge problem of child poverty, with nearly three million children now raised in workless households, many of them by lone parents. Our aims are to:

- **support all families with children, especially poorer families;**

- **help workless parents into the labour market by lowering the barriers to work, especially the lack of affordable childcare;**

- **support working parents;**

- **ensure that financial and emotional support from parents continues even after separation; and**

- **reduce the rate of conceptions among girls aged under 16.**

■ POLICY DIRECTION

Support for families with children

2. The Budget focused resources and policy reform on families. The Chancellor stressed that providing children with a good start in life is the best investment government can make. Extra resources are going to all families with children, but more to those most in need. We believe that additional support should be provided for children in poorer families on the basis of the identifiable needs of children, not on whether there happens to be one parent or two. So there is no case for a one-parent benefit, and the Government will not return to that approach.

3   We have also underlined our commitment to Child Benefit in the Budget. Child Benefit should and will remain universal where it is already universal and should be paid as now, directly to the mother, with an increase in the rate of benefit for the oldest child of £2.50 a week from April next year. Families throughout the country – including those on means-tested benefits – will gain from this investment. It must be right in principle that if Child Benefit is raised in future, then there is a case for higher rate taxpayers paying tax on it.

4   On top of the increase in Child Benefit, those families on income-related benefits will gain a further £2.50 a week for each child aged under 11. This recognises the additional pressures faced by families with younger children and represents a substantial investment of resources to those most in need.

Helping parents into work

5   Having a parent in work provides children with an active, valuable role model. It helps provide the parent with self-respect and a social network. And most important of all, a waged family is less likely to be poor and benefit-dependent than an unwaged one.

6   For those bearing the extra costs of children – and receiving higher out-of-work benefits as a result – the gap between benefit levels and pay levels is often narrow. Indeed, some parents might make their families worse off by working. The Working Families Tax Credit (WFTC) – discussed in more detail in **Chapter Three** – will offer more generous support to working families, reducing the numbers facing high marginal tax rates and improving work incentives.

7   For many families, the cost of childcare is a major obstacle to work. For too many parents, the costs of childcare have meant either that parents cannot afford to work or find themselves paying out most of their wages on childcare. The previous Government attempted to address this problem by introducing a **childcare disregard** in Family Credit. But the disregard has failed to live up to expectations – it has been taken up by just 32,000 families, many fewer than was originally expected. Moreover, it provides no help to the poorest families.

8   The Government's proposed WFTC will therefore contain a generous **Childcare Tax Credit** for low-income working families. WFTC will offer support for childcare through the tax system and make a reality of choice for families previously denied it. The new tax credit will be worth up to 70 per cent of eligible childcare costs, subject to a maximum payment of £70 a week for a family with one child; £105 a week for a family with two or more children. (This compares to a maximum support at present through Family Credit of £42 a week, rising to £70 a week in respect of two or more children from June.) The new limits have been chosen to reflect the average costs of childcare, while also providing an incentive to 'shop around' to find good value.

9 This Childcare Tax Credit is one aspect of our **National Childcare Strategy**. As well as helping parents to meet the costs of childcare, we are working to ensure that all parents who need it have access to good-quality childcare. We will implement this strategy, in consultation with parents and other interested parties, to improve the supply of good-quality, affordable childcare provision in every neighbourhood. We will be publishing a Green Paper after Easter.

10 We will support a national network of out-of-school provision, including childminder networks, which will help up to one million children and their parents throughout the UK over the next five years. We are investing £42 million in the 1998/99 financial year to support the creation of more out-of-school places on top of the 80,000 already created through the Out-of-School Childcare Initiative. Between 1999 and 2003, we will inject a further £260 million from the **New Opportunities Fund** and the **Out-of-School Childcare Initiative** into out-of-school childcare. Bids for the Fund will be invited in early 1999.

11 Through the New Deal, the Government will also offer work experience and training places for up to 50,000 people, helping to increase the numbers of skilled childcare workers in the labour market.

Support for working parents

12 Combining paid work and parenting is a constant juggling act. Being a parent and an employee is not easy and working parents need as much support as possible. Our proposals to improve the quality of childcare are crucial. The Ministerial Group on Family Policy is looking at what more can be done to improve parenting education and support.

13 Children need their parents' time as well as their love and financial support. This is one reason the Government is implementing the *Working Time Directive*, which will limit the hours employers can normally demand of their workers. This will allow working parents to spend more hours with their children. It will give, for the first time, a statutory right to a holiday. The *Parental Leave Directive* will also be applied to the UK, increasing the opportunities for parents of young children to take time away from the workplace, unpaid.

14 Although such policies to promote family-friendly working practices would not traditionally be seen as welfare measures, this Government sees them as being at least as important as changes to the benefit structure.

Modernising child support arrangements

15 Changes in society mean that parental separation is becoming less exceptional. By providing parents, children and families with greater support, our policies may help to stem the tide of family breakdown.

16 But children have the right to the financial and emotional support of both their parents wherever they live. The Child Support Agency (CSA) is intended to ensure that non-resident parents meet their financial responsibilities to their children, but it has failed on a number of counts. Many parents succeed in frustrating the child support scheme: almost a third of fathers who should pay through the collection service are paying nothing. To make matters worse, the complex and bureaucratic system faces opposition from both the person paying and, all too often, the parent providing the bulk of care. Currently, more than two thirds of lone mothers who claim Income Support are seeking to avoid applying for child support maintenance from the fathers of their children.

17 We are looking carefully at all aspects of the child support scheme to see where improvements can be made. We have already identified ways that we can improve the service offered to parents. Lone parents who claim Income Support will be assisted by Benefits Agency staff in completing the application for child support maintenance. This will ensure that they do not have to deal with two separate offices or give information more than once. Our aim is to speed up the child support assessment process. The new decision-making and appeals provisions (of which further details are provided in **Chapter Ten**) will also allow the CSA to increase the effectiveness of its work. We are conducting a 'root and branch' review of the CSA and we will announce proposals for fundamental reform later this year.

Looking after children

18 Some children are not fortunate enough to have the active support of their parents. We recognise in particular that the needs of children looked after by their local authority need to be addressed. The Government will lead a campaign to strengthen the support that local authorities give to children for whom they have a parental responsibility and will be introducing specific measures to provide targeted support to them. For example, we could:

- **issue statutory guidance to authorities and schools;**

- **provide better information on educational outcomes;**

- **promote advocacy schemes to improve educational opportunities; and**

- **require local authorities to continue to remain involved as young people move into further and higher education.**

Reducing teenage conceptions

19 Young teenage conceptions can trigger a cycle of deprivation from which it is very difficult to escape. Life chances can be ruined: educational achievements and employment prospects are likely to be harmed by early and unplanned pregnancies which disrupt the learning process. Teenage conceptions in the UK are among the highest in Europe, and rising. More than nine out of a thousand girls aged under 16 became pregnant in 1996, up from just over seven out of a thousand in 1980.

20 But the risks of early pregnancy differ starkly by geographical area, with deprived communities characterised by higher rates of teenage pregnancy. Comparing rates of teenage conceptions across health authorities, the highest rate is more than five times the lowest. A successful policy to reduce teenage conceptions therefore needs to identify and focus on those parts of the country where it is a particular problem.

21 There is good evidence to show that education is the best defence against early pregnancy. Young women with a good education – and thereby something to lose – are less likely to become pregnant early. So our drive to improve educational standards, described in **Chapter Five**, will play a key role here along with the focusing of resources on poorer areas through the **Education Action Zones**.

22 We are also considering ways of improving education in the specific areas of sex and relationships. Plans are being made to take forward the proposals in the White Paper, *Excellence in Schools*, to teach secondary school pupils about the responsibilities of parenthood. These initiatives are designed to encourage young people to think carefully about their personal and sexual behaviour, and to delay taking the decision to have children until they are ready to cope. A national programme to tackle the problem of conceptions among girls aged under 16 is being developed.

Success Measures

1. **An increase in support from the tax and benefit systems going to families with children.**

2. **A reduction in the proportion of children living in workless households.**

3. **A rise in the proportion of parents meeting their financial obligations to their children, after separation.**

4. **A decrease in the rate of conceptions among girls aged under 16 in the areas most affected.**

Chapter Eight

Attacking social exclusion

Principle Six

There should be specific action to attack social exclusion and help those in poverty.

1 Helping those who are not in a position to help themselves is a mark of a civilised society. Those people for whom work is not an option are entitled to an income which allows for a decent life.

2 For most of the post-war period, the combination of economic growth and the welfare state ensured that most sections of society prospered together. The advance might be compared to a collective train journey. While not everyone was in a first class seat, the whole population moved forward at the same pace and in the same direction. This trend faltered in the last 20 years. The carriages containing the most vulnerable became de-coupled, and fell behind.

3 **Chapter One** described the process of rising inequality in income and opportunities for work. Certain groups have suffered disproportionately from the rising gap between rich and poor – especially children and those pensioners without extra provision for old age. **Chapter Four** described how we propose to help poorer pensioners. **Chapter Seven** set out our measures for tackling child poverty. In addition, particular communities have been hit hard by multiple disadvantages, such as unemployment, poor skills, low income, low-grade housing, high crime, bad health and family breakdown. We call this social exclusion because linked problems effectively shut people and areas out from participation in normal working and social life and access to public services that work.

■ POLICY DIRECTION

Social exclusion

4 This combination of social, economic, educational and other disadvantages in certain pockets requires a new, cross-departmental and long-term policy response. The causes of social exclusion are varied and complex and often cut across traditional Government boundaries. Many of the individuals and communities affected by social exclusion are on the receiving end of many separate public programmes and professional services. The poor rarely have the chance of helping to determine the programme of action for themselves. These programmes are rarely integrated; most deal with symptoms rather than causes; and most have been driven by the structure of existing Government machinery rather than by the needs of citizens. Not surprisingly, these approaches have often been ineffective.

5   The **Social Exclusion Unit** was set up by the Prime Minister to help co-ordinate action across Government; to shift the focus of action away from mopping up after the damage has been done and towards preventing social exclusion from happening in the first place; and to find new and more integrated ways of tackling the worst problems. It demonstrates the Government's determination to tackle social exclusion.

6   In the first phase of its work programme until July 1998, the Unit will focus on three priorities:

- **school dropouts, both truancy and exclusion – looking at how to make a step reduction in the scale of truancy and exclusions from school and to find better solutions for those who have to be excluded;**

- **rough sleeping – looking at ways to reduce the numbers living rough on the streets to as near to zero as possible; and**

- **developing integrated and sustainable solutions for areas facing particularly severe problems, including crime, drugs, unemployment, the breakdown of communities and bad schools.**

7   The Unit will look at a number of other areas, including:

- **integration: improving the way that central government departments, local government and other agencies work together to tackle social exclusion; and**

- **indicators: drawing up key indicators of social exclusion to measure progress.**

8   The Unit will draw on its experiences with these first tasks to make recommendations by May, for targets to tackle in the second half of 1998.

9   In Scotland, a **Social Exclusion Network** has been established consisting of senior officials from the Scottish Office Departments, the Employment Service and the Benefits Agency. A consultation paper was issued in early February and a summit on social exclusion will be held in the spring. These arrangements will enable an approach to be taken towards social exclusion which reflects Scottish circumstances but also takes account of the work of the Social Exclusion Unit in England.

10 In Wales, a network of officials has been established in the Welsh Office, drawing together people from across the range of the Department's responsibilities. This network is currently working up a programme of action, focusing attention at the local level on the need for integrated planning and community commitment, to combat problems of social exclusion in the most deprived communities in Wales. Proposals will take account of the considerable groundwork already underway within local authorities and other agencies: partnership and collaborative working will be a cornerstone of the social exclusion programme for Wales. Detailed proposals will be announced later in the spring.

11 The Secretary of State for Northern Ireland has announced that the **Targeting Social Need** initiative will now include *Promoting Social Inclusion* (PSI) – co-ordinated, cross-Departmental action to tackle social exclusion. While it will take account of the Social Exclusion Unit's work, PSI's agenda, methods and structures will be tailored to Northern Ireland's needs. Consultation with relevant social partners will help to clarify the most appropriate model for PSI and to establish its agenda.

12 The Government has also announced the introduction of a **New Deal for Communities** in order to help provide employment opportunities for those in the worst housing estates. £15 million will be invested in 1998/99 to start pathfinder projects which will inform the development of the full initiative and the wider Government strategy on poverty and exclusion.

Success Measures

1. **A reduction in the scale of truancy and school exclusions.**

2. **Fewer people sleeping rough.**

3. **The introduction of a better model for tackling effectively the linked problems of the most deprived neighbourhoods.**

Chapter Nine

Rooting out fraud

> ### Principle Seven
>
> **The system should encourage openness and honesty and the gateways to benefit should be clear and enforceable.**

1   Fraud undermines the integrity and purpose of the social security system. Taxpayers and genuine claimants support the system on the basis that resources go to those who are entitled, not to those who are dishonest. Most claimants, of course, are honest, but fraud still costs taxpayers and claimants an estimated £4 billion (of which about £1 billion is Housing Benefit fraud), enough to give every family with children an extra £10 a week.

2   While the negative impact of fraud is clear, the nature of fraud is highly complex. Claimants do not have a monopoly on fraudulent activity: fraud is also committed by rogue employers, dishonest landlords or even, on occasion, public sector officials. There is a wide spectrum of fraud, from deliberate misrepresentations made by individuals filling out forms through to organised criminal activity.

3   The Government is committed to tough action to stop social security fraud. Clear and enforceable gateways to benefit are needed if the benefit system is to encourage honesty. Adequate information is vital: claimants are sometimes unaware which changes they have to report, and how. The current range of counter-fraud initiatives lack coherence and vision. We are reviewing all existing counter-fraud arrangements. A group of experts in local government and the private sector have been asked to help draw up a counter-fraud strategy. The work of this group is feeding into the review of counter-fraud arrangements, the results of which will be published shortly.

4   Previous attempts to reduce fraud have concentrated on 'quick wins' – short-term savings which result from fraud detection. Of course, detection is a vital plank of the Government's strategy, and we will be developing improved monitoring systems as well as improving sanctions, using powers in the Social Security Administration (Fraud) Act 1997.

5   But in the long-term, the most cost-effective approach is to prevent fraud from occurring in the first place, by designing more secure and accurate benefit systems through a more inclusive approach to benefit design and delivery.

6   Our three-pronged campaign against fraud therefore consists of:

- **improved detection;**

- **more effective deterrence; and**

- **better prevention.**

■ POLICY DIRECTION

Improved detection

7   The Government's strategy is to shift the emphasis away from detection towards preventing fraud from occurring in the first place. But there remains a need for resources dedicated to the investigation and detection of fraud. We want to inject a new professionalism into this work, with better quality training, the attainment of professional qualifications and the publication and dissemination of good practice.

8   The Government is already working with local authorities to develop effective solutions to Housing Benefit fraud. We are conducting an extensive review to establish a fuller picture of the extent of Housing Benefit fraud. We have given authorities financial incentives to improve their counter-fraud activity and introduced **new legislation** to give them greater powers to tackle fraud by landlords. Local authorities can now obtain more information from landlords, control direct payments more tightly and recover overpayments more easily.

9   A new **Housing Benefit Matching Service**, which matches local authority data with that held by other local authorities, is being phased-in nationally and is due to be fully operational by December 1998.

10 Organised fraudulent activity by groups of landlords often takes place across council borders, making detection more difficult. Local authorities in London, with Department of Social Security support, have therefore set up a **cross-council specialist team** against organised Housing Benefit fraud. We will be evaluating the work of this team closely to see if there are lessons for local authorities in other areas.

11 In order to improve detection of fraud by employers who evade National Insurance liabilities, earlier this year we launched a **Business Anti-Fraud Hotline**.

More effective deterrence

12 Once a fraudulent payment or series of payments has been detected, the sanctions triggered should be fair and appropriate. Recent legislation will enable the Government to crack down more effectively on fraud. Effective and appropriate penalties may help to deter others from attempting to de-fraud the system, if publicised successfully. But the most effective way to deter individuals from fraud is to improve the chances of detection.

13 We will make use of a **broader, more flexible range of penalties** to enhance the measures presently available. Until recently, criminal prosecution was the only sanction available, apart from recovery of overpaid benefit; but court actions are costly and in many cases not in the public interest. The Department of Social Security and local authorities can now use powers in the Social Security Administration (Fraud) Act 1997 to impose a financial penalty as an alternative to prosecution.

14 The Act also created a **new criminal offence of dishonest misrepresentation**. And powers in the current Social Security Bill will improve the range of sanctions against employers and individuals who evade National Insurance contributions.

15 Effective deterrence also requires a change in general attitudes. A parallel example is the campaign against drink-driving which has gradually altered public perceptions of the crime. We will launch a **presentation and publicity strategy** to make sure that people receiving benefits are clear about their responsibilities and to reinforce the message that fraud harms not just an anonymous system, but the whole community.

Better prevention

16 Permanent reductions in the level of fraud can only be achieved by better prevention. The first step towards preventing fraud is to build a clearer picture of which benefits are vulnerable to fraud, which individuals are most likely to commit fraud and which systems are most open to abuse. Then appropriate steps can be taken: for example, the mechanisms affecting the most fraud-prone benefits can be revised to reduce the opportunities to commit fraud. In this way, we will move towards designing fraud out of the system.

17 We are changing processes within Government to achieve this. Systems will be built to identify and assess the risks of losses from fraud. For example, we are producing a **Verification Framework** to help local authorities check Housing Benefit claims more effectively at the outset and prevent fraud from occurring.

18 This will require better use of information and intelligence. Information sharing is critical to effective prevention, and will be promoted by the Social Security Bill. We are already piloting **better computer links** between the Department of Social Security and local authority Housing Benefit offices, which will help to prevent fraud and overpayments, as well as improving the administration of Housing Benefit and Council Tax Benefit. For example, an officer in a Housing Benefit office will be able to check the information on a claim with the same individual's records at the Benefits Agency, so that discrepancies – deliberate or accidental – are picked up before the claim is processed.

19 And we are examining the feasibility of a **National Intelligence Unit** in the Contributions Agency to gather and analyse information to target investigative work more effectively. The Unit's work would continue after the transfer of the Agency to the Inland Revenue.

20 To prevent the abuse of National Insurance numbers, a thorough validation of the National Insurance Records System will be undertaken, building on the work already underway to improve its integrity.

21 We have widened the remit of the **Benefit Fraud Inspectorate**, launched in November 1997, to provide an over-arching, long-term view of activities. Through its inspection programme, the Inspectorate will monitor the effectiveness of counter-fraud activities across all areas of social security and promote inter-agency collaboration.

22 This Inspectorate will also spread best practice and help with the examination of the scope for improving benefit design and systems to prevent fraud. In line with our commitment to openness in Government, all of its reports will be published.

Success Measures

1. Clearer gateways for eligibility.

2. Greater transparency about entitlement and costs.

3. A reduction in the amount of money lost in fraudulent payments.

4. A reduction in the number of incorrect payments.

Chapter Ten

A modern service

> ### Principle Eight
>
> **The system of delivering modern welfare should be flexible, efficient and easy for people to use.**

1. Social security customers and jobseekers have the right to good quality, convenient and responsive services which both help them with their individual needs and enable them to fulfil the obligations which go with receiving benefits. In some areas we are already a long way down this road. Recipients of Jobseeker's Allowance already receive a one-stop service from Jobcentres, delivered jointly by the Employment Service and the Benefits Agency, which concentrates on helping them back to work as well as paying their benefits. This gives us a model on which to build.

2. But in many other areas, the way social security is delivered has not kept pace with rising expectations of service quality. Services are too often passive, not active, with the emphasis on paying out money rather than helping as many people as possible fulfil their potential and achieve independence. Those who provide education and health care services, who deliver benefits, and help with training, with jobsearch, and childcare arrangements, are central to our plans to reinvent welfare. Yet they do not always have the tools at their disposal which help them to help people.

3. Customers and staff tell us that they want changes to the way social security services are delivered. They are fed up with duplication, inefficiency, red tape and unnecessary complexity. Customers and taxpayers want improved services; they do not want money wasted on artificial barriers and inefficient processes. The Government is responding to that demand for change and listening to ideas and suggestions. We are determined to build an **Active Modern Service** to meet the needs and expectations of customers.

4. This chapter describes the component parts of a modern, ACTIVE service:

- **A**ctive services, helping those people who are able to move towards work, and helping those not in a position to work to achieve the best quality of life possible.

- **C**ustomer-focused services which meet customers' needs, rather than those of the organisations delivering services.

- **T**ransformed services, which employ modern methods which are easier for customers to use, for example, better information technology.

- **I**ntegrity and security against fraud to be built into the system.

- **V**aluing staff and giving them the support they need to provide a quality service.

- **E**fficient services which ensure that organisations work in partnership to deliver effective, customer-focused services.

■ POLICY DIRECTION

Active services

5   Many people are able to find their own way into work immediately after leaving education or after they have lost a job. Others need more help. We plan to provide customers with **personal advisers** who can actively help people move from welfare into work.

6   Personal advisers will help to identify skills and training needs; they will help find work placements, training and education. Where there are barriers to work, for example, a lack of childcare, they will work with customers to overcome them. They will ensure that the move from welfare to work is as smooth as possible, that benefits continue uninterrupted, where necessary, and that support remains in place even after the customer returns to work.

7   In some areas we are already putting this into practice. In the New Deal for Young People, those entering the programme now have a personal adviser who works with them to identify their employment and training goals and ensures that they receive the support of partner organisations and specialists when they need it. Personal advisers will get to know their customers in depth and use their skills and expertise to help them back to work. In a very similar way, the New Deal for Lone Parents has personal advisers working with every lone parent, to offer them individual guidance, advice and counselling.

Satisfied Lone Parents and Young People on New Deal Programmes

Quotes from lone parents in New Deal trial areas:

"It's about time the Government did something to help people better themselves and help them get off benefit. I feel like I've been trapped for so long and it's fantastic to be able to come here and talk to someone who genuinely wants to help me change my life and help me go down the path I actually want to go down." (North Cheshire)

"I would still be sitting at home thinking about work if you hadn't contacted me. I think it's a great idea, you have been really helpful." (North Cheshire)

> Quotes from young people in New Deal pathfinder areas:
>
> *"The chance to be listened to as an individual and equal, not just a faceless ticket number, was greatly welcomed by me, no doubt others as well."* (Cornwall)
>
> *"I have signed on for years and this is the best service I have ever known. I feel like you are giving me a real opportunity to make something of myself."* (Southern Derbyshire)
>
> *"New Deal is the best thing to happen to this country for years."* (Northern)

8   For those people who are unable to work or who have retired, active services will mean that customers receive the right kind of help with the process of claiming benefits and that benefit payments are made promptly and without hassle. Customers will not have to worry about dealing with more than one Government agency – the barriers and boundaries will be managed for them.

Customer-focused services

9   People want a user-friendly benefit system. They want simpler ways of getting information and claiming benefits, that are not bound up by red tape and lengthy, cumbersome forms. They often want to contact us by telephone, so they can speak straight away to a person who can give them the advice they need. The Benefits Agency, for example, already provides the **Benefit Enquiry Line** for disabled customers who wish to contact them by telephone, which offers advice on benefit entitlement and help for those who have difficulty completing their claim forms. Within the Employment Service, we are currently piloting arrangements enabling employers to notify job vacancies, and jobseekers to access them, by telephone in the evenings and at weekends. Equally, many customers need to be able to sit down with a member of staff and discuss their problems on a one-to-one basis. Services need to reflect the specific needs of the individual, as well as the general needs of the many.

10 One major obstacle claimants often face is duplication: they have to give the same information many times over, to different parts of the organisation. A lone parent's details might need to be entered into five different computer systems by four different agencies (Benefits Agency, Child Support Agency, Contributions Agency and local authority). As far as possible the benefits system should seem to customers to be a single service.

11 One way of delivering a customer-focused service is to improve infrastructure and information technology systems so that information is processed and used more effectively, following the example of banks and insurance companies. New ways of working will provide customers and staff with information that is up-to-date and accurate. The Social Security Bill currently passing through Parliament contains **powers for data-sharing** that will make this possible.

12 The Bill also contains measures to **simplify and streamline decision-making and appeals** in social security and child support. Having better-informed customers, who provide more accurate and complete information in support of their claims, will help us get more decisions right first time. And any errors which are made will normally be rectified without the need to go through a legalistic and cumbersome appeals process.

13 The Government is replacing the existing five tribunals for appeals with a single, unified tribunal. This will ensure consistency and make the system easier to understand for customers and staff. We are committed to reducing the waiting time for an appeal, which currently averages six months. Tribunals will also be given the powers to correct their own errors, avoiding automatic, time-consuming referral to the Social Security Commissioners. We will set challenging targets for dealing with appeals and Parliament will receive an annual report on whether those targets have been achieved.

14 We are determined to help people claim their benefits more easily by replacing the existing paperchase with a simpler, clearer system. We are developing a **new claim form** which will be tested on a small number of lone parents shortly. Rather than having to plough through 90 pages of questions to apply for benefit and child support maintenance, we will guide the customer through a condensed form which is tailored precisely to the individual's circumstances. We have also introduced a system for pensioners to complete their claim forms by giving information over the telephone. And we are reviewing all our written material to ensure that information is presented clearly and comprehensively.

Transformed services

15 As part of the drive towards electronic government, we are experimenting with a range of new technologies to improve services. We have pledged that 25 per cent of government services will be available electronically by 2002. In the first half of this year, we will be piloting new software to speed-up the processing of claims from some lone parents, by dealing with their child support maintenance applications, as well as their claims for Income Support and Housing Benefit, in one go. Over the longer term, electronic access points, Internet services and video links are all possibilities. We are also looking into the case for an electronic claim form.

16 In place of the multiple records we have to keep now – one for each benefit – we are moving towards a new information technology infrastructure with a single, up-to-date record for each customer. Then we can provide the one-stop services customers expect of a modern welfare state.

17 We have also piloted **kiosk technology** in Cambridge, which allows customers to use touch screens placed in benefit offices to get information on job opportunities as well as benefits.

> ### Kiosk Technology in Cambridge
>
> The Benefits Agency has been working in partnership with Opportunity Links (a voluntary organisation), the County Council and the private sector to set up an information service on the Internet. The site is accessible to anyone with an Internet connection – in libraries, cafés, Benefits Agency offices, at home or work.
>
> The service provides up-to-date information and advice on childcare, training and jobs throughout the county. There are sign-posted links to and from the Department of Social Security website, giving easy access to benefits information.
>
> The service is popular with customers, as this extract from a phone conversation with a Benefits Agency member of staff demonstrates:
>
> *"How do you find the kiosk?"*
> "It's really easy...really simple. No problem getting round it at all."
> *"What about the information? Did you find it useful?"*
> "Yes – I've just got a job from it. I'm starting on Monday. It's worked for me."

18 In the Employment Service, a number of experiments are underway allowing unemployed people to access vacancies directly in Jobcentres through touchscreens. The initial reaction of customers has been very favourable.

Integrity

19 Cutting out waste and duplication and ensuring that taxpayers' funds are properly spent and accounted for are all essential to winning public confidence in the modernised welfare state. It is crucial that we cut out fraud and build a system with integrity, as **Chapter Nine** showed. Providing a modern service means ensuring that money is paid only to those who need it, so that we will be able to afford to spend more on active services tailored for individuals.

20 We have learnt several lessons from the current Disability Living Allowance Benefit Integrity Project which may apply more widely. It is clear that at any single point in time some benefit payments are not correct. This is often because customers do not know what changes they need to tell us about, or because we do not respond swiftly enough to any change in their circumstances. We are looking at ways to give customers regular opportunities to update us and ensure that they know what changes to report, and when.

21 We will be testing some **joint services** with the London Borough of Lewisham and local Benefits Agency offices, which will include some joint visits to customers who are currently required to give broadly the same information, on two separate occasions, to staff from each organisation. In addition, better liaison with the Inland Revenue and Customs and Excise can bring services together for employers.

Valuing staff

22 While greater use of technology will be very important, it cannot substitute for well trained and motivated staff delivering services knowledgeably and sympathetically to customers. We must not lose sight of the fact that the dedication and ethos of our front line staff – often doing a difficult job in demanding circumstances – is one of our greatest assets. We aim to work with staff to develop a new public service ethic appropriate for a proactive service which seeks to combine the best public and private sector practice. The growing role for personal advisers exemplifies this new approach.

23 We want staff to take pride in delivering a quality public service. Successful reform needs the support and confidence of those at the sharp end. Staff will be given the training and the systems they need to carry out new roles. Equally we will look to them for views on how to improve the service we provide. For example, last summer the Benefits Agency held a series of workshops and discussions around the country. The resulting comments and suggestions have helped to shape the development of new policies and working practices.

Efficient services

24 Finally, we must break down the artificial boundaries between departments and organisations, in order to offer a simple, efficient service. At a local level, this means more effective working between Benefits Agency offices, Jobcentres and Housing Benefit units in local authorities so that social problems can be addressed comprehensively. Welfare is not simply a matter of paying out cash, but includes every aspect of people's lives: education, employment, health, housing, transport and so on. We aim to work with other organisations – including voluntary bodies – to tackle the wider issues, not just the narrow aims of the benefits system.

25 New partnerships are already springing up. For example, the Department of Social Security and the London Borough of Camden are working together to pilot the new lone parent claim form described above. One staff member will help a lone parent to apply for all benefits and child support maintenance without having to traipse between offices. This will allow lone parents who want to work to concentrate on searching for a job rather than worrying about when their payments will be made.

26 More widely, the Government is determined to improve the public services for older people. The Cabinet Office is leading a consortium to work with older people to give them more say in how public services are run, as well as simpler access to services and better information on their rights through a series of pilot projects beginning in June.

27 The focus will be on how services can be provided in a seamless and user-friendly way for frail elderly people. Different approaches will be tried out, including improving links between hospitals and social services departments, new one-stop schemes, and mobile services.

A vision for the future?

- **As the Active Modern Service develops, the contact points between services and customers will change and diversify. We welcome views on the merits of the possible approaches.**

- **In the future, customers will be able to access services:**

from home:

- People will routinely get information or advice by making a telephone call or by using the Internet. Visits to an office will be confined to the cases where customers really need to see our staff face-to-face or staff need to see them.

- Better integration of Government services will make it easier to deal with a wide range of issues through a single point of contact.

- People may be able to keep in touch with their personal advisers by telephone, e-mail or even by video link.

from public access points:

- Public access points, perhaps with built in video links, may be available in a wide range of public places: on the high street, in community centres, leisure complexes or shopping arcades. Especially in remote, rural areas, it may become far more common to talk to staff by phone or even video conference than to make the trip to the nearest town.

from offices:

- While our staff will still need to have a clear focus on the rights and responsibilities of customers, they will also have access to information across a whole range of public services and will be able to give people a much more comprehensive service.

Success Measures

1. An increase in the level of customer satisfaction.

2. An increase in the proportion of customers who regard the service as personalised and tailored to their individual needs.

3. An increase in the public service ethos and an improvement in job satisfaction and achievement amongst those working in welfare services.

4. An increase in collaboration between the Employment Service and Benefits Agency to promote jobs not benefit dependency.

5. A reduction in duplication between agencies, to maximise value for money, making best use of new technology to deliver services.

Chapter Eleven

The fourth age: Welfare 2020

1. The previous chapters have set out the principles that will guide reform of the welfare state into the Third Age. They demonstrate that our ambition is nothing less than to:

   - **restructure the institutions of welfare in order to promote people's opportunity and independence; and**

   - **protect the vulnerable so that everyone can enjoy a secure and dignified life.**

2. The purpose of this chapter is to provide an impression of what some elements of the welfare state might look like in the year 2020 when the reform process is complete and we step into the Fourth Age of the welfare state. It sets out:

   - **the *values* that will underpin 'Welfare 2020';**

   - **the new *welfare contract* between state and citizen;**

   - **the different *mechanisms* through which welfare might be delivered;**

   - **the sources of *funding*; and**

   - **the *success measures* which will guide our reform programme.**

Values

3. Welfare 2020 will be built on three core values of work, security and opportunity, in line with our principles set out in this Green Paper.

4. Our reform programme will be based on these values. In the process of reform we will be:

   - **consulting widely and listening to what people themselves want;**

   - **judging carefully how the reform programme should be adapted in line with people's views; and**

   - **maintaining continuous progress towards a new system solidly based on the principles we have outlined.**

Welfare Contract

5   At the heart of the modern welfare state will be a new contract between the citizen and the Government, based on responsibilities and rights.

Towards a new welfare contract

Duty of Government:	*Duty of individual:*
• Provide people with the assistance they need to find work. • Make work pay.	• Seek training or work where able to do so.
• Support those unable to work so that they can lead a life of dignity and security.	• Take up the opportunity to be independent if able to do so.
• Assist parents with the cost of raising their children.	• Give support, financial or otherwise, to their children and other family members.
• Regulate effectively so that people can be confident that private pensions and insurance products are secure.	• Save for retirement where possible.
• Relieve poverty in old age where savings are inadequate.	• Not to defraud the taxpayer.
• Devise a system that is transparent and open and gets money to those in need.	

Duty of us all:

- To help all individuals and families to realise their full potential and live a dignified life, by promoting economic independence through work, by relieving poverty where it cannot be prevented and by building a strong and cohesive society where rights are matched by responsibilities.

6   The development of the new contract will lead to greater:

- *Trust* – with a clearer contract, people can have greater confidence that they will get proper protection in return for the contributions they make.

- *Transparency* – the new welfare contract will make it much clearer what benefits people are entitled to, and what conditions they have to meet to get those payments.

- *Responsiveness* – a more transparent system will be a more responsive one. As people understand more clearly the nature of the welfare contract, they will want more information and a greater say over how their payments into the system are being used.

- *Responsibility* – greater responsiveness and improved information will reinforce the enhanced sense of responsibility that lies at the heart of the new welfare contract, with people not only taking more personal responsibility for their own and their families' wellbeing, but also more collective responsibility for policing the new system and preventing fraud.

- *Empowerment* – as people take up the opportunities to work and become more independent.

Mechanisms

7   We envisage that in the Fourth Age, welfare will be delivered through three channels:

A modern service – increasingly focused on giving people the chance to be independent and meeting their individual needs. Our plan is for a single work-focused gateway into the benefit system for all those of working age who can work, providing customers with a flexible, professional, personalised service. In particular, we envisage personal advisers helping claimants develop a tailor-made action plan for regaining their independence. We will work with the private and voluntary sectors to find innovative ways of delivering welfare and helping people into jobs. Increasingly, the services delivering help with jobs and welfare will need to work more closely with other local agencies. In addition, we will work to ensure that everyone can access high-quality on-line information about job and training opportunities, while also making their details available to employers. For people unable to work or retired, the new service will ensure they receive their benefits on time.

Services – our new emphasis on preventing poverty will mean that more of the welfare state will be delivered through high-quality services – education, health, job assistance, childcare – and less on social security payments.

Mutuals and private providers – In 2020, these providers will deliver a substantial share of welfare provision, particularly pensions.

Funding

8   With people living longer, it is inevitable that provision for retirement will increase. We expect that much of this increase will be delivered by private and mutual providers and that the proportion of the welfare budget funded by the tax payer will not increase. We would expect government spending to give greater emphasis to measures which prevent poverty, such as education and health, as more people move into independence and off benefit.

Success measures

9   The effectiveness of our reform programme will be judged against the success measures set out in this Green Paper. Welfare reform is, by its nature, a long-term process. The Government is determined to set long-term aims to guide its reforms over the next decade and beyond. The full list of the eight principles and associated success measures follows.

> **Principle 1: The new welfare state should help and encourage people of working age to work where they are capable of doing so.**

1   A reduction in the proportion of working age people living in workless households.

2   A reduction in the proportion of working age people out of work for more than two years.

3   An increase in the number of working age people in work.

4   An increase in the proportion of lone parents, people with a long-term illness and disabled people of working age in touch with the labour market.

> **Principle 2: The public and private sectors should work in partnership to ensure that, wherever possible, people are insured against foreseeable risks and make provision for their retirement.**

1. At the end of the process of reform, there should be a guarantee of a decent income in retirement for all.

2. An increase in the amount of money going towards savings and insurance, but without increasing the proportion borne by government.

3. An extension in high-quality second-tier pension provision to a greater proportion of the working population.

4. An increase in public confidence in the quality and regulation of private sector savings, pensions and insurance products.

> **Principle 3: The new welfare state should provide public services of high quality to the whole community, as well as cash benefits.**

1. An improvement in the health of the population as a whole by increasing the length of people's lives and the number of years they spend free from illness.

2. An increase in the proportion of 11 year-olds with good literacy and numeracy skills and a reduction in the number of school leavers with no recognised qualifications.

3. An increase in the proportion of the adult population with educational qualifications.

4. An improvement in the quality of housing and housing management.

> **Principle 4: Those who are disabled should get the support they need to lead a fulfilling life with dignity.**

1. A reduction in discrimination against disabled people.

2. An increase in the number of disabled people able to work.

3. A reduction in spending on Incapacity Benefit, as the number of claimants falls, with more resources available to help severely disabled people with the greatest needs.

4. A simpler, clearer and fairer system for determining entitlement to disability benefits.

Principle 5: The system should support families and children, as well as tackling the scourge of child poverty.

1   An increase in support from the tax and benefit systems going to families with children.

2   A reduction in the proportion of children living in workless households.

3   A rise in the proportion of parents meeting their financial obligations to their children, after separation.

4   A decrease in the rate of conceptions among girls aged under 16, in the areas most affected.

Principle 6: There should be specific action to attack social exclusion and help those in poverty.

1   A reduction in the scale of truancy and school exclusions.

2   Fewer people sleeping rough.

3   The introduction of a better model for tackling effectively the linked problems of the most deprived neighbourhoods.

Principle 7: The system should encourage openness and honesty and the gateways to benefit should be clear and enforceable.

1   Clearer gateways for eligibility.

2   Greater transparency about entitlement and costs.

3   A reduction in the amount of money lost in fraudulent payments.

4   A reduction in the number of incorrect payments.

Principle 8: The system of delivering modern welfare should be flexible, efficient and easy for people to use.

1 An increase in the level of customer satisfaction.

2 An increase in the proportion of customers who regard the service as personalised and tailored to their individual needs.

3 An increase in the public service ethos and an improvement in job satisfaction and achievement among those working in welfare services.

4 An increase in collaboration between the Employment Service and the Benefits Agency to promote jobs not benefit dependency.

5 A reduction in duplication between agencies to maximise value for money, making best use of new technology to deliver services.

Appendix

The evolution of social security

The birth of state provision

1. The first significant steps towards our social security system were taken exactly four centuries ago, with the **Elizabethan Poor Laws** of 1598 and 1601. These laws established founding principles which shaped development into the present century.

- **The state – through local parishes – had a responsibility to prevent destitution, to raise taxes to do so and to establish an administrative framework for action.**

- **In delivering assistance, a distinction was drawn between people who needed support because they were unable to work, and people who were capable of self-support but jobless.**

- **Assistance was not a right: especially for those of working age, it was subject to conditions of behaviour.**

2. The Poor Laws envisaged that the so-called deserving poor unable to work would be maintained and cared for in almshouses, many of which over time gradually evolved into public hospitals. People capable of work were in principle expected to obtain help only by attending workhouses. In practice, other methods of support developed over time. In addition to maintenance within the workhouse itself, a system of 'outdoor relief' paid allowances, in cash and in kind, to the needy – both elderly and unemployed – in their own homes. Rural employers took on quotas of unemployed workers. The sons of pauper families were sometimes placed in apprenticeships. And in some urban areas with high concentrations of unemployed people, there were also active measures to tackle worklessness at its roots by creating self-financing 'pauper manufacturies'.

Wages and welfare – Speenhamland

3. The basic assumption of the Elizabethan Poor Laws was that people with work did not need assistance. It was not until the late eighteenth century that the problems of low-income workers began to be recognised. In 1795, at a time of rapid price inflation, magistrates at **Speenhamland** in Berkshire sought to prevent distress among working families through a system of poor relief which offered wage top-ups to poor labourers, with amounts linked to family size and changes in the price of bread. Although, the 'Speenhamland system' was much criticised by later Victorian thinkers, it addressed an important problem in social security: the effect of family size on costs and standard of living.

4   Around this time there were also experiments with other approaches to the same problem. For example, the effect of family size on income began to be recognised through child allowances in the newly-born income tax system. Unsuccessful attempts were also made to introduce child payments for those on low incomes.

Provider of last resort: the New Poor Law

5   An important change of direction occurred in 1834, following the report of the **Royal Commission on the Poor Laws** established two years earlier. The Commission was greatly opposed to cash assistance for the working poor, and took the view that dependency on the state must be discouraged by harsh measures. Its key recommendation was that people supported by the parishes should not enjoy the same lifestyles as workers; in the language of the time, they should be 'less eligible' than even the poorest labourer. Outdoor relief for the able-bodied should be abolished and the only place where help was available should be the workhouse, access to and conditions within which were to be made deliberately harsh. In a break with parish autonomy, many rules of the **New Poor Law** were set centrally, although they were still interpreted and administered locally.

Self-help and voluntary organisation

6   During the nineteenth century a number of new forms of social provision developed, partly as a response to the harsher Poor Law, partly because of the very strong Victorian self-help ethic and partly because of the changes brought about by the Industrial Revolution in employment conditions and urbanisation. The development of friendly societies, co-operative savings associations and trade unions – the self-help movement – cannot be separated from the growing belief among nineteenth century working people that they had the power within themselves, and from the organisations they built, to create the opportunities for genuine self-improvement. Membership of friendly societies rose from under one million in 1815 to seven million – almost the whole of the working population – by 1892.

7   But this impressive statistic concealed two problems. Many workers, although members of mutual societies, could contribute little or could not keep up their contributions regularly. Their benefits were often no more than a death grant to prevent a pauper's funeral. Moreover, the friendly societies themselves were constituted to deal with short-term interruptions in employment rather than with the long-term demands of old age. A series of friendly society bankruptcies at the turn of the century showed that neither low-wage workers nor their societies could afford benefits for retirement. Although poverty remained widespread at this time, it tended to be concentrated among the elderly.

8   Alongside the mutual institutions, the Victorian era also saw flourishing charitable and voluntary activity. In the second half of the nineteenth century, the resources available to the charities in London alone exceeded the amounts spent in official

poor relief. However, although this assistance was often ill-focused and its delivery had a strong moral imperative: '*We must use charity to create the power of self-help*', it did help to highlight contemporary issues such as cleanliness, temperance and public health which benefited poorer workers.

Work as the best form of welfare

9   The slump of the 1880s began to break the Victorian belief that self-help was sufficient and that only motivation was wanting among the poor. A number of social surveys, culminating in the pioneering work of Charles Booth and later Seebohm Rowntree, analysed the causes of deprivation and quantified the extent of poverty for the first time. Politicians also began seriously to set themselves the task of dealing with unemployment. In 1886, Joseph Chamberlain, in his capacity as President of the Local Government Board, broke new ground by issuing a directive to local poor law guardians urging a new kind of assistance. He proposed the development of useful work schemes, for which wages rather than poor relief would be paid, with safeguards against dislocating existing workers. Although this initiative did not take off, it indicated a changing climate of opinion.

10 Further steps towards an active labour market policy came with the establishment of labour exchanges – early job centres – in 1905. These helped to combat unemployment by matching workers with vacancies. Five years later, under Winston Churchill, the exchanges were brought under national control and became centrally funded. Churchill's Trade Boards Act of 1909 also laid the foundation for minimum wages in vulnerable industries.

The road to old age pensions

11 The work of Booth and Rowntree from the 1880s onwards confirmed the extent to which poverty was a problem of old age. They showed that of all those dying over age 65, half would be relying on the Poor Law in their last years. Yet only one in nine would have had recourse to poor relief at all before the age of 60. In the face of these statistics it was difficult to maintain either that poverty was a limited problem of personal inadequacy or that it could be coped with by voluntary effort – at any rate for the elderly. State intervention was needed.

12 A number of different schemes were discussed by reformers before finally, in 1908, the Liberal Government came forward with a plan for a non-contributory pension. Implemented from January 1909, this 5 shillings 'Lloyd George Pension' was payable from age 70, equally to men and women. Although subject to a means test administered by local pension committees (and initially also a test of good character), it was enthusiastically received by the elderly as an alternative to the punitive conditions of the Poor Law. The Government had estimated that the scheme would cost between £6 and £7 million. By 1914, the actual costs had already almost doubled to £12.5 million. This compared with only £2.5 million paid to the elderly in poor relief, an indication of its inadequacy and the extent to which life expectancy was improving.

National Insurance: sickness and unemployment

13 The reforming Liberal Government, inspired by the example of Germany, next turned its attention to sickness and unemployment. The **1911 National Insurance Act** hammered out a compulsory health insurance scheme which welded together all interests. Workers and employers paid compulsory flat-rate contributions. 'Approved' friendly societies administered minimum cash benefits which could be topped up by additional contributions to the societies themselves. And an Exchequer contribution bought in rights for workers not previously insured through a friendly society. Although administratively complex, the scheme was the first example of social protection achieved through a flexible partnership between the state and non-state providers. It lasted for 37 years, until superseded by the introduction of the NHS and the strictly state-funded Beveridge scheme of 1948.

14 Alongside sickness benefits and run in a similar way, the 1911 Act also introduced a world first – contributory unemployment benefits for high-risk industries prone to trade fluctuations.

War and depression

15 The next staging posts in the development of social security were prompted by the First World War and its aftermath of economic depression and mass unemployment. War pensions, essentially unchanged today, were an immediate consequence of the war and a Ministry of Pensions was set up to deal with them in 1917. Unemployment insurance was extended in 1920 to almost all workers below a certain level of annual income, and in 1925 pensions for widows and orphans were created. In the same year, contributory retirement pensions for those aged 65 and over were tacked on to the existing non-contributory scheme.

16 The reforms of the first quarter of the century had primarily been driven by the need to find an alternative to the deterrent Poor Law for respectable working men and women. By the late 1920s, economic recession and rapidly rising unemployment meant that large numbers were exhausting their time-limited entitlement to contributory benefit and becoming reliant again on local poor relief. A series of increasingly desperate measures to extend contributory benefit in anticipation of future contributions could not be sustained, despite cuts in benefit levels and the exclusion of married women from benefit. But politically it was not acceptable to allow a million unemployed men to fall back on the Poor Law. A new approach was needed.

17 The **1934 Unemployment Assistance Act** created a two-tier system of contributory unemployment benefit for the first six months followed by a centrally administered and consistent means-tested benefit for as long as necessary. Thus for the first time an entire class of people was taken out of the ambit of the locally administered Poor Law. Also, for the first time, central government took on responsibility for determining an equitable subsistence rate in a variety of different circumstances, rather than simply setting a flat-rate amount. This represented a massive increase in the complexity of the state's involvement in welfare provision.

18 The 1934 Act also established the **Unemployment Insurance Statutory Committee**. One of the duties of the Committee was to monitor the financial position of the Unemployment Fund and make recommendations to the Government on contribution and benefit rates. The Government was not obliged to follow these suggestions; but it was obliged to work within the financial parameters set by the Committee. Beveridge, who was made chairman, turned this Committee into a powerful body of civil society.

The Beveridge Blueprint

19 By the early 1940s, most of the key elements of social security were in place in some form. Contributory benefits existed for old age, sickness, unemployment and widowhood. There was a national safety-net for the unemployed, extended in 1940 to embrace the elderly also. But benefits and conditions were disparate, nine different central departments were involved and there was no coherent approach to common issues such as the presence of dependants. Sir William Beveridge, who had already had a lifetime's association with the problems of unemployment, was commissioned to consider improvements. His powerful report, published in November 1942, became an instant bestseller and a crucial influence on social policy right up to the present day.

20 Beveridge's strength was not primarily as an innovator but as a synthesizer, able to bring together a series of disparate benefits within a single coherent framework and impose a rationale which has stood the test of time. He aimed to replace the existing separate schemes with a unified system of social insurance, based on flat-rate benefits in exchange for a single flat-rate contribution and covering the whole population, rather than (as previously) only lower earners. Insurance benefits would be wholly financed by the state and the link with the friendly societies broken. At the same time, they would be extended to cover all general insurable contingencies – not just old age, widowhood, unemployment and sickness but also birth and death. Provision for dependants was made consistent, and a centrally administered scheme of National Assistance would provide means-tested additions on a common basis where there were additional needs.

21 The central aim of Beveridge's plan was to provide a basic subsistence income during all those contingencies which interrupt earnings. He did not take account of the problems of non-workers or the special needs of disability, something which was later to be seen as a gap in his vision. However he did recognise the importance of shoring up in-work incomes for families with children, who might quickly find pay falling below benefit level plus dependants' allowances. His plan therefore was predicated on the introduction of Family Allowances for the second and subsequent child in any family regardless of means and payable both in and out of work. (The first child was excluded because "*It is reasonable to assume that one child at any rate can be maintained from family earnings.*") Family Allowances were introduced in August 1946, as the first truly universal benefit.

22 Despite the influence of Beveridge's ideas, some of the key principles of his system were not adopted by the post-war government, mainly on account of cost. Beveridge had envisaged that insurance benefits would be set at a level sufficient to provide an acceptable minimum income, with only rare recourse to means-tested National Assistance. He had also believed that Family Allowances too should be set at subsistence level. The Government's White Paper, *Social Insurance*, Cmd 6550 (1944) rejected both these propositions. It argued:

"Social insurance must necessarily deal in averages of need and requirement. It cannot adapt itself to the almost infinite variety of individual conditions. Circumstances vary, not only between places, but between people, and the conception of relating individual payments precisely to individual needs is not really capable of realisation in an insurance scheme... The right objective is a rate of benefit which provides a reasonable insurance againstwant..."

23 The National Government also overruled Beveridge's recommendations in another important respect. He had envisaged that rights to the new-style contributory retirement pension would build up over time as contributions accrued. Conscious that a third of elderly people were now receiving means-tested help from the Assistance Board, the Government took the decision to introduce pensions immediately at the full rate. On 5 July 1948 – 50 years ago this year – the welfare state came into being.

The Beveridge inheritance

24 Changing economic and social circumstances have rendered many of the details of the Beveridge plan out of date or thrown up new issues to grapple with. But the lasting importance of his work has been not so much in the detailed prescriptions as in the powerful vision he presented of the *possibility* of common action to defeat the giants of '*Want, Disease, Ignorance, Squalor and Idleness*'. He saw clearly – and inspired others to see – that financial support is not sufficient by itself to tackle the problems of poverty and distress. As he pointed out, Disease often causes Want, '*Idleness...destroys wealth and corrupts men*', whilst '*Ignorance...no democracy can afford among its citizens*'. Social security, in his view, should be one aspect only of this wider vision.

Two nations in old age

25 The enormous hopes which were vested in the 1948 welfare state meant that the UK entered the post-war era with a belief that the problems of poverty had been solved. By the late 1950s it was apparent that this was not the case. The difficulties focused on how to deliver an adequate income in retirement.

- **The levels of the flat-rate benefit did not provide sufficient income to maintain an elderly person who had no other income.**

- **But the centralised and standardised structure did little to encourage people to make additional personal savings.**

26 Although Beveridge had never envisaged that his scheme would provide incomes above a minimum – and had been at pains to stress the importance of additional provision – the post-war welfare debate moved into a new phase. The question was not just whether there should be benefits to prevent poverty, but benefits sufficient to maintain a higher standard of living in retirement. Scarcely ten years after the welfare state began, serious political consideration was again focused on provision for old age – with the aim this time of providing a retirement income linked to previous earnings.

27 An interim step was taken in 1961, with the introduction of **Graduated Insurance contributions** which purchased modest additional pension. But this scheme was much more orientated towards relieving pressure on the National Insurance Fund than towards improving benefits. The major issue which consumed a further 17 years of vehement debate was the proper role of private and occupational pension provision in providing a retirement income above the flat-rate level. Partly because of the perceived inadequacy of the state pension and partly because of improving economic conditions, the membership of occupational pension schemes began to creep up during the 1950s and 1960s, reaching 12.2 million by 1967. This increasing supplementary provision fuelled the difficulties of improving the general scheme, by pointing an ever-increasing contrast between those with and without an extra pension.

28 Two abortive attempts failed to reach the statute book before finally the **State Earnings Related Pension Scheme (SERPS)** was implemented in 1978. This ambitious scheme aimed for the first time to yield a total pension income at retirement of around half average earnings, by providing a substantial earnings-related element on top of the basic flat-rate pension. Where employers provided a good occupational pension, their employees could be 'contracted-out' of the earnings-related element of the pension in return for a rebate of contributions. Those without occupational provision received the additional pension from the state. The scheme also included important measures to address the problems of those with interrupted employment, in particular carers.

29 Although these arrangements took a significant step away from the pure state provision of the Beveridge plan, they still emphasised a predominant role for the state, especially in guaranteeing the value of pensions in payment. During the 1980s and early 1990s, successive changes were made, partly to cope with concerns about the heavy future costs of SERPS, partly to increase individual choice by enabling individuals to contract out on a personal basis into individual money purchase pensions, and partly to deal with the consequences of European legislation on equal treatment for men and women. Further changes reflected the increased need to protect those who changed jobs and to address concerns about the security of occupational pensions in the wake of the Maxwell affair. This led to legislation, culminating in the **1995 Pensions Act**, which established an equal state pension age of 65 to be phased in between 2010 and 2020, strengthened the regulation of occupational pensions, and altered the terms for contracting out of SERPS.

Sick and disabled people

30 The focus in Beveridge's plan on dealing with interruptions in earnings meant that he did not seriously confront the problems of long-term sickness and disability. By the early 1970s, concern over the dependence of disabled people on means-tested assistance prompted the creation of a series of new benefits which broke the social insurance mould in every way. People unable to work because of serious disabilities or because of caring for others became entitled to receive income maintenance benefits as of right, regardless of income or of contribution record. And for the first time social security benefits became payable to help meet some of the extra cost of living for people who needed care or had serious mobility problems. These developments broadened the role of social security considerably, helping to redress inequalities as well as simply to maintain basic income.

31 Alongside these new benefits in the 1970s, basic insurance provision for the long-term sick was also expanded considerably. The level of benefit for people sick for over 26 weeks was increased, and by 1980 the levels of long-term benefits such as Retirement Pension and Invalidity Benefit were 25 per cent higher than for 'short-term' benefits such as Unemployment Benefit. Extra amounts were added for age, as well as an earnings-related element similar to SERPS. The effect of these developments was to increase dramatically both the number of recipients and the duration and cost of their stay on benefit. Reforms in 1990 and 1994 cut back the additional amounts and tightened the conditions of access.

32 Although state support for long-term sick and disabled people increased substantially from the 1970s onwards, support for short-term sickness began to move in the opposite direction. The growth of occupational sick pay schemes meant an increasing overlap between Sickness Benefit and employer support and made state provision less necessary. A series of measures from 1982 onwards began to withdraw from direct state provision in this area, instead placing obligations on employers to pay Statutory Sick Pay, and later Statutory Maternity Pay.

Family support

33 Beveridge had envisaged that problems of incentives for people in low-paid work, and the extra difficulties of families with young children, could be met by a flat-rate Family Allowance payable for the second or subsequent child in a family. This existed alongside child tax allowances. For financial reasons Family Allowances were not increased as other benefits rose, and by the late 1960s it became evident that a high proportion of low-income households consisted of families in full-time work, few of whom could benefit from child tax allowances. Over a nine-year period successive Governments attempted four different approaches to the problem:

> - increasing family allowances for low-income families whilst reducing tax allowances for others;
>
> - introducing Family Income Supplement, as a means-tested earnings top-up for low income families in work;
>
> - publishing proposals for a tax credit scheme; and
>
> - introducing universal Child Benefit, which in 1979 replaced both Family Allowance and child tax allowances.

34 During the 1980s, the growth of lone parenthood and family breakdown tested the social security system in new ways and in particular increased the numbers of lone parents reliant on out-of-work means-tested benefits. The expansion of **Family Income Supplement** in 1988 to create **Family Credit** aimed to encourage more families into work and ensure that they would always be better off working than not working. Family Credit now provides extra income to three-quarters of a million families, but at the price of a continuing overlap between the tax and benefit systems.

Means-tested benefits

35 The 1948 reforms established a coherent National Assistance scheme – covering both maintenance needs and housing costs – alongside the newly-reorganised National Insurance system. Although the means-tested benefits were paid according to consistent national scales, access to them was not a legal entitlement.

36 The creation of **Supplementary Benefit** in 1966 attempted to make the system more open, accessible and fair. This provided a legal entitlement to the basic personal scale rates whilst discretion continued for allowances to meet extra needs. By 1974 over a third of recipients were receiving extra payments. A process of reform, begun in the late 1970s, and implemented in 1980, tried once again to simplify the system by codifying a range of weekly additions and one-off payments for reasons such as heating or diet, making some of them automatic, (for example, where a child was aged under 5), and setting the entitlement conditions in regulations. This regulated approach led to greatly increased costs. In 1988 the present Income Support arrangement of personal allowances and automatic broadbrush premiums for family needs, age and disability was introduced. The creation of **Jobseeker's Allowance** in 1996 merged contributory Unemployment Benefit into this integrated structure.

37 The **National Assistance and Supplementary Benefits** schemes provided that recipients should have their housing and local taxation costs met in full. Those with income just above the limit, or who did not qualify for some other reason – for example, because the head of household was in full-time work – received no assistance. In 1967 a national scheme of rate rebates was introduced to provide

some relief for people on low incomes who were not receiving Supplementary Benefit. In 1972, this was extended to provide rent rebates and allowances also. The schemes were not part of the social security system and were administered by local authorities, answering to the then Department of the Environment.

38 **Housing Benefit** was introduced in 1983, replacing rent rebates and allowances and responsibility for the new benefit moved alongside other income support. During the last decade, increases in Housing Benefit expenditure have focused attention particularly on rent levels in the private sector. Overall, the number of individuals in households dependent on at least one of the major means-tested benefits doubled over the period since 1979 – from one in six to one in three.

Lessons for the future

39 This account of the development of social security picks out only the highlights of change. Since 1948 there have been over 120 Acts of Parliament and many thousands of pieces of subordinate legislation continuously amending the system in major and minor ways. It has not all been a story of growth – some areas have greatly reduced in significance, and some responsibilities have ceased altogether. But on the whole social security in the 1990s attempts to cover a far wider range of wants and pressures than were ever contemplated by the Liberal reformers of 1911 or by Beveridge and the post-war Labour Government. Yet all this has taken place within the lifetime of the oldest pensioners.

40 What conclusions should be drawn from the past?

- **Reform is not a new challenge for social security. It is the norm. Each generation since the turn of the century has seen major shifts in the direction of social provision. There have been at least nine different answers for pensions alone.**

- **The effects of change in social security are unpredictable. Within five years the first old-age pensions cost twice as much as expected. When pensioners were given access to a non-stigmatised means-tested benefit in 1940, four times as many as expected claimed in the first year. The disability and care benefits introduced in the 1970s have grown massively beyond original expectations.**

- **The scope of welfare has continually expanded as national income and people's expectations have increased. The big issue at each stage of welfare's development has been how best to meet the cost.**

- **There is no permanent solution. The same problems of incentives, of the balance between state and private provision, of how to support families, have faced every stage of social security development. The challenge of welfare reform is how best to strike this balance in today's and tomorrow's special circumstances.**

Printed in the UK for The Stationery Office Limited on behalf of the
Controller of Her Majesty's Stationery Office
Dd 5067997 3/98 77240 Job No 44168